STEREOSCOPIC PHENOMENA OF LIGHT & SIGHT

by Theodore Brown

A Guide to the Practice of Stereoscopic Photography
and its Relation to Binocular Vision.

A Digest of Stereoscopes and Stereoscopic Appliances,
together with some particulars of the
Stereoscopic Industry in Great Britain and America.

New Introduction by David Starkman & Susan Pinsky
Biographical Notes by Stephen Herbert

Facsimile of 1903 Edition

Reel 3-D Enterprises, Inc.
1994

This book is a facsimile of an original 1903 copy. Readers interested in historical accuracy should note that in the original edition the half-tone plates were printed separately on "art paper" and appeared in the book without page numbers, and with a blank page on the back of each plate. For economy we have left out the blank page, but inserted the plates facing nearest the page they did originally. This will explain the gaps in numbering and the changing placement of odd/even page numbers. The original hardcover was a dark green cloth with black lettering – impossible to reprint, so we have created a new cover for this edition.

First Printing – 1903 by The Gutenberg Press, Ltd., London
Second Printing – January 1994 by Reel 3-D Enterprises, Inc.
(Second Printing Limited to 1,000 copies)

New Introduction Copyright ©1994 by
Reel 3-D Enterprises, Inc.
P.O. Box 2368
Culver City, CA 90231
U.S.A.
Tel: (310) 837-2368

ISBN 0-939617-01-3

Printed in the United States of America

INTRODUCTION

The first question that came to our minds in writing a new introduction to a book first published in 1903 is "Why bother?" When we first discovered this book a few years ago we had already been involved in 3-D photography for 15 years, as photographers, publishers, and merchants, yet we had never heard of Theodore Brown nor his book. As we read the book, however, we began to feel more and more that this would be a book of great interest and value to modern stereo photographers and historians. Although the film formats may have changed, and most (not all!) modern stereo photographers use slide film, the basic techniques and background that Brown put into print have remained remarkably the same.

At the same time it is interesting to look back and see how this subject was approached more than 90 years ago, and to see how much, and yet how little, has changed. Today we take our camera equipment (even 3-D camera equipment) so much for granted that we are content to compose and shoot without stopping to think about the underlying phenomenon of stereoscopic vision, how it works, and what mechanical and technical goals have to be achieved to make it all successful. As a photographic inventor Theodore Brown did contemplate these questions and *Stereoscopic Phenomena of Light and Sight* was the result. It is interesting to note that he did not title his book "Stereoscopic Photography Techniques" or something similar.

Later we learned why it is not surprising that we had not heard of Theodore Brown. *Stereoscopic Phenomena of Light and Sight* was published in a very limited quantity of perhaps 500 copies, and it is estimated not more than 1,000. The copy from which this facsimile is made is hand numbered No. 307. Our sincere thanks to David Burder, London, for making his original copy available to us.

We also would know nothing of Theodore Brown, the man himself, had it not been for his other interests in Magic Lanterns and early Cinematography. Because of this, Stephen Herbert of the Museum of the Moving Image, London, recently gave a lecture on Theodore Brown, and he was kind enough to provide a brief biography for this edition. After 91 years of obscurity we are very pleased to resurrect Theodore Brown's book on stereoscopy and make it available to contemporary 3-D enthusiasts. We hope you will enjoy & benefit from this book as much as we have.

–David Starkman & Susan Pinsky
Culver City, California, January 1994

THEODORE BROWN

Theodore Brown was born in 1870 in Salisbury, England. He trained as an engraver, but soon developed a passion for photography. His special interests were stereoscopic pictures and the magic lantern. From his mail-order "Stereoscopic Supply Stores" he sold mirror attachments that enabled ordinary cameras to take stereoscopic pictures. He also experimented for many years with projection systems - still and movie - for viewing stereo images without glasses. (He refers to this on the title page of this volume, "INVENTOR OF DIRECT STEREOSCOPIC EFFECTS ON THE OPTICAL LANTERN SCREEN") - but despite returning to the challenge throughout his life, he failed to produce a commercially viable result.

In 1902 he married Bessie Moore, (shown playing the piano in Plate 4), and *Stereoscopic Phenomena of Light and Sight* was published the following year. Brown purchased the defunct *Optical Lantern Journal* (previously the *Magic Lantern Journal*) in 1903, and publishing resumed in 1904 as the *Optical Lantern and Cinematograph Journal*. Early in 1907 it became the *Kinematograph and Lantern Weekly,* the film trade's first periodical, and Theodore Brown stayed on as Editor for a year or two before taking up other pursuits. ("The Kine Weekly" finally died about 1970. *The Magic Lantern Journal* was revived in 1978 by the Magic Lantern Society, and is still going strong).

After a brief spell living in Bournemouth, where Theodore published "Magic Postcards" (anaglyph postcards with tear-off 3-D glasses attached) and a catalogue of "Stereoscopic Specialties," the Browns moved to London in 1907. Theodore was active in many areas of work, including early movie technology. He designed and patented many children's toys and optical novelties, including the Spirograph home projector for showing movies from a celluloid disc.

With the failure around 1930 of his final attempt at a "3-D movies without glasses" system, he concentrated on paper engineering, designing ingenious and innovative models for a successful range of children's pop-up books. Theodore Brown died in London in 1938.

–Stephen Herbert
  Museum of the Moving Image
  London, 1994

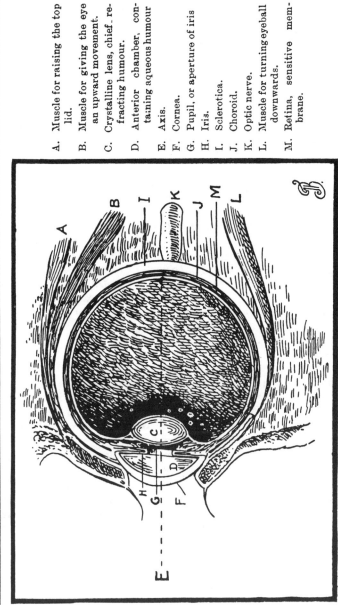

A. Muscle for raising the top lid.

B. Muscle for giving the eye an upward movement.

C. Crystalline lens, chief refracting humour.

D. Anterior chamber, containing aqueous humour.

E. Axis.

F. Cornea.

G. Pupil, or aperture of iris

H. Iris.

I. Sclerotica.

J. Choroid.

K. Optic nerve.

L. Muscle for turning eyeball downwards.

M. Retina, sensitive membrane.

Vertical Section of Human Eye, looking from the posterior side of the left eye.

STEREOSCOPIC PHENOMENA

OF

LIGHT AND SIGHT:

(1st Edition)

BY

THEODORE BROWN,

INVENTOR OF

DIRECT STEREOSCOPIC EFFECTS ON THE OPTICAL
LANTERN SCREEN.

―――

A GUIDE TO THE PRACTICE OF STEREOSCOPIC PHOTOGRAPHY
AND ITS RELATION TO BINOCULAR VISION.

A DIGEST OF STEREOSCOPES AND STEREOSCOPIC APPLIANCES,
TOGETHER WITH SOME PARTICULARS OF THE
STEREOSCOPIC INDUSTRY IN GREAT BRITAIN AND AMERICA.

―――・◆・―――

Illustrated with 16 Half-tone Process Plates and upwards of
100 Line Drawings.

―――・◆・―――

" The Kaleidoscopic designs of nature, never
presenting the same pattern twice, yet
constituted of a given material; inspires
the constructive mind that brings a new
invention."

―――

The Gutenberg Press, Ltd.,

123-5, FLEET STREET, LONDON, E C.

1903.

INTRODUCTION.

THE operation of agreeably exciting the senses of man is a subtle process of nature difficult to imitate, but once her laws have been discovered, a close adherence thereto will enable the artist with camera or brush to execute copies which shall, as often as looked upon, give pleasure. The extent of such pleasure will, of course, be according to the number of refining qualifications the product may contain ; and the excellencies to which we now refer are not necessarily found in nature, but more often may be traced to the mind of the artist labouring to express the ideal of his thoughts.

This complex reflection of natural phenomena with the utterance of the soul, claims the sympathy of the world ; and whilst expressive of the individual medium through which it is conveyed, reminds the beholder of a boundless universe of which he forms a part.

Though it must be conceded that our best imitations of nature are but echoes and shadows of the real ; that our recreations fall short in force or beauty of that we heard, or saw ; yet it is well that we should imitate ; for, when somewhat of the natural survives, we like the copy and call it good.

Now the fundamental principle on which the science and art of stereoscopy is based, is such that a medium is here provided, through which the nobler thoughts and feelings of the artist's soul may be revealed, with exactly that poise between definiteness and vagueness in which they were conceived. This communicative channel is moreover unique in that it makes possible the permanent retention of natural phenomena, in a manner so comprehensive and minutely true, that the original impression may be preserved and passed for ever onward.

To those who have hitherto regarded solidity or relief in the stereoscope merely as an optical illusion, a curiosity, or as the final and highest aim of the stereoscopist, these claims may seem extravagant ; a more serious reflection, however, will suffice to show that this double art (as we may call it) opens a gate to fields of beauty otherwise unapproachable, and fascinating at every step the explorer with new discoveries.

PREFACE.

In compiling the present volume, it has been the aim of the author to avoid as much as possible a repetition of previously published facts relative to the science and art of stereoscopy; with the hope that his work may merit the qualification of being a necessary addition to the literature on the subject.

The analogy that exists between the laws of binocular vision and the rules for stereoscopic photography, has been dealt with at some length; a digest given, of stereoscopes and stereoscopic appliances; phenomena of light and sight; together with some notes on the commercial side of stereoscopy. For convenience of reference the line diagrams have been inserted near to the text to which they refer, whilst in order to secure the best possible impressions from the half-tone blocks, these have been printed upon art paper and inserted as plates.

ACKNOWLEDGMENTS.

_____

My best thanks are tendered to the publishers of " The Photographic Art Journal," "The Amateur Photographer," "Photography," " Photographic News," " The British Journal of Photography," "The English Mechanic," and "The Dioptric Review," for services rendered by the loan of blocks and giving permission to reprint portions of articles contributed by the author to their various publications.   Also to Mr. Tylar, of Birmingham, and especially to the Gutenberg Press, who have by their kindness greatly facilitated the work of preparing this volume.

MIDSUMMER, 1903.   Number of this copy...*304*

CONTENTS.

(See Index at end of Book.)

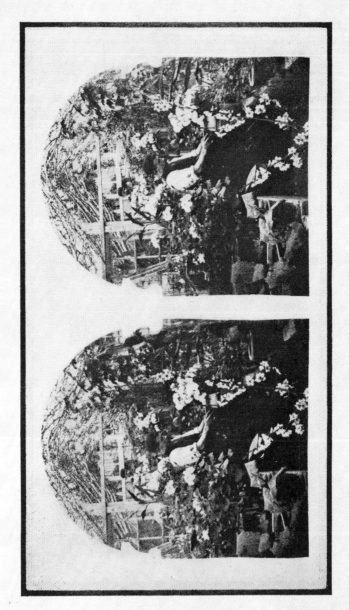

The effect of looking through a window, produced by masking.

PLATE 1.

PART I.

OUR EYES AND STEREOSCOPIC PHOTOGRAPHY.

 HE idea conveyed to the mind whilst viewing a landscape in nature with both eyes, is that of a single impression, but on closer investigation it is found that such a sensation is really the product of two distinct retinal impressions simultaneously conveyed to the mind through the optic nerve. We cannot attempt to describe the precise way in which this wonderful performance takes place, although we have sufficient knowledge of the eyes' optical system to enable us to say with certainty how the eyes move by muscular control, and adapt themselves for distinct vision.

It is not surprising that from our infancy up we have been accustomed to regard the double impression of binocular vision as single, when we remember that many of the changes which take place in our eyes are involuntarily performed. We might mention, in passing, the instinctive contraction of the iris as the eye is brought under the influence of excessive light, and its dilation or enlargement of the pupil as the light decreases. Again, the modification in shape of the chief refracting humour, the crystalline, as distant and near objects are successively observed; and, finally, that mysterious reference of retinal impression to the brain. When we begin to consider what is necessary in a pair of retinal pictures, in order to give relief in the stereoscope, we are of necessity driven to a careful study of the eyes.

So similar is the work accomplished by means of the photographic camera to that of perceiving an object with the eye, that the latter has been compared with the former, but we are inclined to think that a reversal of such comparisons would serve to show how some makers have wandered in the design of their instruments from this more perfect refractor of light. And we say this, not forgetting that the eye is not strictly achromatic and efficiently corrected for spherical aberration. This noble organ of sight, termed, as it has been, "a complete world of wonders," offers for our investigation an inexhaustible store of optical agreements. Though the student of physiology may be confronted here with problems difficult of solution, and the optician observes strange phenomena beyond his powers of explanation, the stereoscopic enthusiast may yet find a general knowledge of its structure and use of material assistance in practical work.

It was said by the great American, Emerson : " The virtue of art lies in detachment, in sequesting one object from the embarrassing variety. Until one thing comes out from the connection of things, there can be enjoyment, contemplation, but no thought. It is the habit of certain minds to give an all-excluding fulness to an object, the thought, the word ; that for the time is made the deputy of the world. These are the artists, the poets, the orators, the leaders of society. The power to detach, and to magnify by detaching, is the essence of rhetoric in the hands of the orator and the poet."

How applicable are these words of Emerson to the wonderful performance of nature within the human eye. As the varying degrees of light impinge upon its surface, there is ever a graceful response to its influence, the mechanism detaching for the time being the object of immediate attention from its less important surroundings, instinctively giving an all-excluding fulness to that object, thus carrying home to the mind of the observer a clear and comprehensive impression of what he sees.

Hence, the photographic artist who desires success in every sense of the word, must of necessity make himself acquainted not merely with the natural powers of light upon the visual organs, and the manner in which the retina of the eye is stimulated, but he must also know the relation existing between such effects, and the sensation it is possible to produce in the mind of the observer when viewing a photographic production.

The Extent to which a Single Picture may Give the Sensation of Relief.—If we make a small hole, $\frac{1}{8}$-in. diameter, in a piece of paper and hold it about eight inches from the eye, and look at some distant object through it, we shall find that whilst the distant object is clearly seen, the image of the hole in the paper is indistinct. Then by turning the attention from the remote plane to a point on the edge of the hole, we shall be conscious that a change has taken place. Whilst the edge of the hole is now clearly defined, the image of the distant object

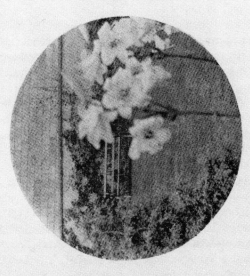

FIG. 1.
Picture upon the retina of the eye when the
attention is directed to the nearest object.

PLATE 2.

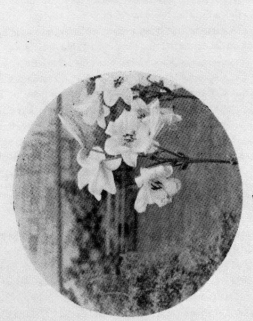

FIG. 2.
Picture upon the retina when the attention is
directed to a remote object.

becomes blurred, so much so that had we not previously observed the nature of the distant object we could not say what it consisted of. The foregoing experiment, which, of course, is conducted with one eye only, is very convincing, and perhaps needs no further remarks to prove that the eye is subject to a change of its focal adjustments; but the accompanying illustrations, Figs. 1 and 2, Plate 2, are interesting examples of retinal impressions that will serve to show other facts in reference to the changes to which the retinal picture is subject, under the influence of accommodation. From these examples we shall observe that not only do near objects become blurred on the retina when the eye is adapted to the remote plane, as in Fig. 2, but also that their magnitude is considerably reduced. Moreover, that when the eye is again accommodated to the near plane, the image of the object in the immediate foreground becomes larger than before, and that remote objects present a larger appearance though they are indistinct. All objects represented in a picture, whether it be a photograph or a painting in oil or water-colours, are of necessity situated at one distance from the observer's eye, *i.e.*, on the surface of the paper or canvas; it is obvious, therefore, that accommodation of the eye will never be needed once the picture has been placed at a suitable distance away. This observation leads us to the question, What plane or particular object in the composition should be most clearly defined in order to give the most realistic effects? The question is essentially a wide one, and its answer must vary according to the subject in hand. In portraiture in the studio it seems the general rule to have the subject in focus and the surroundings somewhat softened off by having them out of focus. In most instances this would be the most natural and, therefore, most agreeable arrangement, as, of course, the object is to direct the attention more especially to the subject, and not to its surroundings, which are of minor importance. For example, we may turn again to our illustration, Fig. 1, Plate 2. If we gaze upon this picture for some moments, and with one eye closed, we shall find that the natural tendency is to turn the axis to the lilies in the foreground, and instinctively the mind appreciates these as the chief objects in the view. As the attention is thus rivetted to this plane, the distant objects are seen only by oblique rays, and a sensation of relief is produced. The fact is, we have here conditions as near to Nature as a single picture, in black and white, can possibly be, namely, the objects of immediate attention sharply defined, and all others, more or less out of focus, according to their supposed distance from the observer's eye. The truth of these remarks is further proved if, after examining the picture with only one eye for some. moments, we suddenly open the other eye, allowing the axes of both to be centred in the lilies. We are at once made aware of the fact that, although some objects are clear and some indistinct, all are at one and the same plane, whilst our photograph is nothing more than a flat surface upon which is depicted varying degress of high and low lights. In other terms we might say that the second eye informs the mind of the plane at which all objects are in reality situated, *i.e.*, at one plane; so that as far as the viewing of a single picture is concerned, we may advantageously dispense with the use of one of our eyes, for, as we have shown, the realistic effects in a single picture are considerably reduced when binocularly considered. It would be drifting from our subject to dwell at length on the proper way to view a single picture, but we might say in passing, that sensations, such as originally experienced

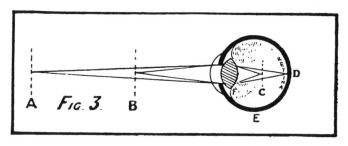

by the artist as he viewed the landscape in Nature, may only be gained from his copy by examining it, not merely with one eye only, but also with the eye the exact distance from the picture as that in which the artist's was situated as he painted it.

Roughly speaking, the eye may be regarded as an optical instrument, based on the principle of refraction. The humour known as the crystalline lens (shown at F in the accompanying diagrams, Figs. 3 and 4), is the chief medium for collecting and transmitting to the retina rays of light emanating from every luminous object before it, so that whilst a large number of pencils are received through the pupil they are all brought to a focus upon the retina, whence the impression is carried by the optic nerve to the brain. The diagrams, Figs. 3 and 4, give a sectional view of the eye in its two separate adjustments for distinct vision of objects at a near and a remote plane. When the retinal picture corresponds in definition to Fig. 1, the constitution of the eye will be similar to that shown in Fig. 3. The lens F will be considerably convexed in order to bring to a focus upon the retina, objects situated at the near plane B. Whilst it is so adjusted the focus of the lens F will be too short for objects at a remote plane A, so that they will be indistinctly seen, the clear image of them being within the eye at C. The moment the observer directs his attention to the remote plane, a change will instinctively take place, and its adjustment will be as shown in Fig. 4, the pupil having dilated, the muscles relaxed, and the lens become flattened, and therefore of longer focus. The images of remote objects will now be sharply projected upon the retina, whilst near objects cannot be distinctly seen because they are not brought to a focus soon enough to be projected upon the retina, but carried beyond, to D, behind the eye. We have said enough to show that natural effect in a single picture may be increased by adding to proper proportion, per-

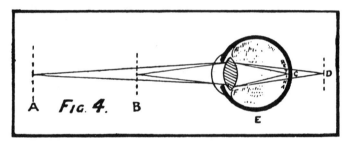

spective, and shade, judicious modification in definition, and if we carry this principle into our work of preparing dissimilar pictures for the stereoscope, we shall not only add beauty to our composition, and effect to its relief, but it will lie within our powers to direct the observer's attention to whatsoever object or plane we desire.

Axial Accommodation of the Eyes.—In addition to accommo-modation of the refracting humours, by which is meant the focusing of the optical system for clear projection upon the retina; in binocu-lar vision this adjustment is supplemented with other changes in-volving divergence and convergence of the eyes' axes. When a col-lection of objects is viewed with both eyes at the same time, con-vergence and divergence of the axes are continually taking place in order that the axes may meet at that point or plane where the object of immediate attention happens to be situated, viz., in Fig. 5, 2 being the object of immediate attention, the axes of both eyes are turned to that point. Any other object situated at the same plane, 4, 2, 5, will also be clearly projected upon the retina. If, for instance, an object is situated at 5, its image will be seen at 5 in each eye, a point upon the retina the same distance to the left of the axis in each case. Any

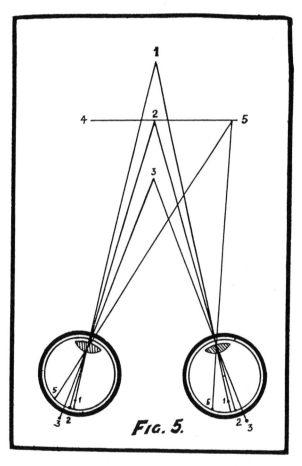

FIG. 5.

object situated at any plane removed from 4, 2, 5, will be seen double and indistinct—double because the rays emanating therefrom fall upon contrary parts of the retina, and indistinct because the constitution of the refracting media is unsuited for any other distance than for the plane 4, 2, 5, viz., with the eyes converged upon 2, as in Fig.

5, rays emanating from the remote object 1 will, in the left eye, strike the retina at a point to the right of the axis, whilst rays from the same object will fall upon the retina of the right eye at a point

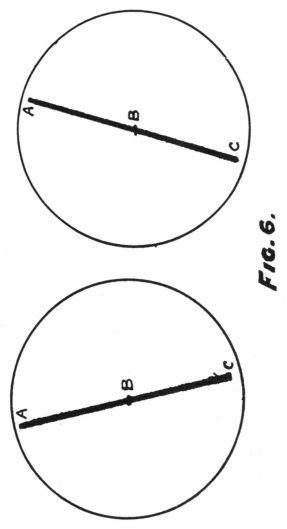

FIG. 6.

to the left of the axis. The same may be said of a foreground object 3, but instead of the image being to the right of the axis in the left eye, it will be to the left of the axis, and in the right eye instead of the image being to the left of the axis it will be to the right. Now, the reason that a sensation of relief is obtained from a pair of dissimilar photographs in the stereoscope, is that the conditions just mentioned are to some extent fulfilled, *i.e.*, being taken from two separate standpoints equal to the separation of the eyes, they present to the mind a double perspective peculiar to binocular vision, with the result that only one plane is seen single at the same moment. To prove this, we may select one of the leading lines in a stereograph of a long narrow lane, and we shall have a diagram similar to Fig. 6 (the perspective here has been slightly exaggerated so that the effect may be very pronounced). On examining Fig. 6 in an ordinary stereoscope, we shall find that it has the appearance of a long bar, with the end C nearest to the observer's eyes. If we direct the attention to the opposite end, A, and fix the attention there, by oblique rays emanating from other portions of the picture, we shall notice that the opposite end, C, does not fall on corresponding parts of the retina in the two eyes, so that it is seen double, and the result will be an

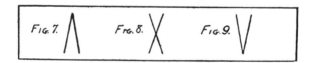

image of the shape shown in Fig. 7. If now we slide the axes of the eyes along the bar towards us, when they cross at the point B we shall see an image similar to Fig. 8. Continuing to converge the eyes' axes till the point C is reached, by fixing the attention here we shall find that the combined image presents the appearance of the letter V, Fig. 9. From such observations we see that the principle of the stereoscope and stereoscopic views is more or less in accord with the laws of binocular vision, as far as it creates an artificial demand for a change in the direction of the eyes' axes, and so we observe there is a close relationship between the laws which govern binocular vision, and those controlling the perception of relief in the stereoscope.

We have already shown that the sensation of relief produced in the mind under conditions of binocular vision, arises from two distinct retinal impressions made by light emanating from the same source, but received at two separate points of view. It is by substituting the human eyes with a pair of photographic cameras that it becomes

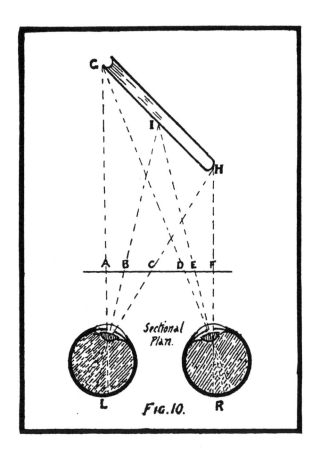

Sectional
Plan.

FIG. 10.

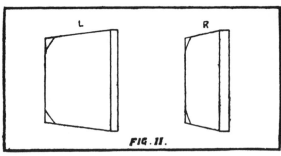

FIG. II.

possible to register more or less accurately upon one plane dissimilar pictures which, when coalesced in the stereoscope, will create an artificial demand for axial changes of the eyes (but no accommodation of their foci), and which will produce a similar relief to that observed when looking at the objects in nature.

This will be easily understood by reference to the accompanying diagram, Fig. 10. Let G, I, H represent a book held obliquely in front of the face. Though the three points G, I, H, are actually at different distances from the observer's eyes they will, when reduced to one plane on the retina of the eyes—on the sensitive plate of the camera—or taken at the line A, B, C, D, E, F, make dissimilar pictures as shown in Fig. 11, in which L is the picture for the left eye, whilst R is the picture for the right eye. Now, if these two pictures be superimposed either by refraction, reflection, or by controlling the muscles of the eyes so that each looks only at its respective picture, solidity will be produced.

Before passing on, it should be noticed that, whilst an artificial relief is thus created, we cannot claim the illusion to be perfect ; for in Nature, whilst the axes of the eyes are turned to the centre point I, Fig. 10, the extreme edges G and H will be more or less out of focus ; whereas the pictures of the book L and R, Fig. 11, will in the stereoscope be the same distance from the eyes at all points considered, and therefore permanently in or out of focus according to the adjustment of the apparatus when the pictures were taken.

Before we proceed to consider the apparatus necessary for successful stereoscopic work, it will be as well to note the peculiar motion of the eyes as a collection of objects are being examined. It is important to observe that the points at which binocular images pass through the pupils to the retinæ vary in separation, according to the distance of the object or objects from the observer's eyes, thus : in Fig. 12, let L R be eyes of normal separation. When a remote object is under examination, the distance between the centres of the pupils will measure $2\frac{1}{2}$ inches ; but when the eyes' axes are directed to a very near object, the distance between the centres of the pupils will measure only $2\frac{3}{8}$ inches. This change, though slight, should not be overlooked, for upon due allowance for this axial movement depends much of our power to make stereoscopic pictures natural or otherwise.

The Stereoscopic Camera.—From our previous observations it is clear that the particular distance between the two points from which a stereoscopic view should be taken, is by no means a matter of taste. On the contrary, it is clear that absolutely natural results may only be achieved by strict conformity to those laws which govern binocular vision. In the branch of photography with which we are now dealing,

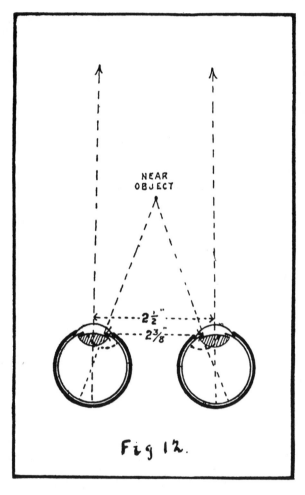

Fig 12.

there has been, and still exists, erroneous ideas as to the proper separation for a pair of stereoscopic lenses. It should not be imagined that by increasing the separation and thereby securing a greater relief in the stereoscope, that additional beauty has been secured; for, if we examine more minutely dissimilar pictures so obtained, we shall soon discover that our perspective have thereby been falsified, and that images of various objects have been distorted, to say nothing of the difficulty experienced when endeavouring to coalesce corresponding points in the stereoscope. We shall have more to say in reference to exaggerated relief later.

Our present diagrams illustrate apparatus that may be termed " the exact binocular camera," whilst the reproduction, Fig. 16, Plate 3, will give the reader some idea as to the quality of work such an apparatus is capable of turning out.

As will be seen, the exact binocular camera is really composed of two instruments placed side by side and pivoted at A-A to a baseboard J. When the cameras touch each other at the back, as shown in Fig. 13, the axes of the lenses run parallel at a separation of $2\frac{5}{8}$ inches. The mechanism provided enables the axes to be converged to a greater or less extent according to the distance of the object to be photographed. A support, G, fastened to the baseboard is fitted with a thumb-screw, F, which passes through a block, I. As the screw, F, is turned, its thread working in the block causes the latter to rise or fall as the case may be.

In the production of a stereoscopic photograph there is more scope for the display of artistic ability than there can ever be in the work of making a single picture : if, however, the operator desires at each exposure of a plate to make a binocular picture, and not merely a slide for the stereoscope, he must make up his mind to use a stand camera, and he must be prepared to spend both time and trouble in the selection and taking of the subject. Under some conditions the use of a stand would of course be out of the question, and a hand instrument, or no instrument at all can be used. In such cases a camera similar to the one we have just described, but without the tripod, might be used. When the camera takes the form of the usual magazine for holding a dozen or so plates, and there is no screen at the back, an axes indicator, shown at R and Q, Fig. 15, must be provided. By means of this indicator the distance at which the axes of the lenses cross may be determined, so that both may be centred upon the object to be photographed without reference to the position of the object upon a screen. Thus, suppose the estimated distance of the object is 12 feet, the thumbscrew, F, is turned till the pointer, R, slides along the scale-plate, Q, and arrives at a number or letter corresponding to that distance.

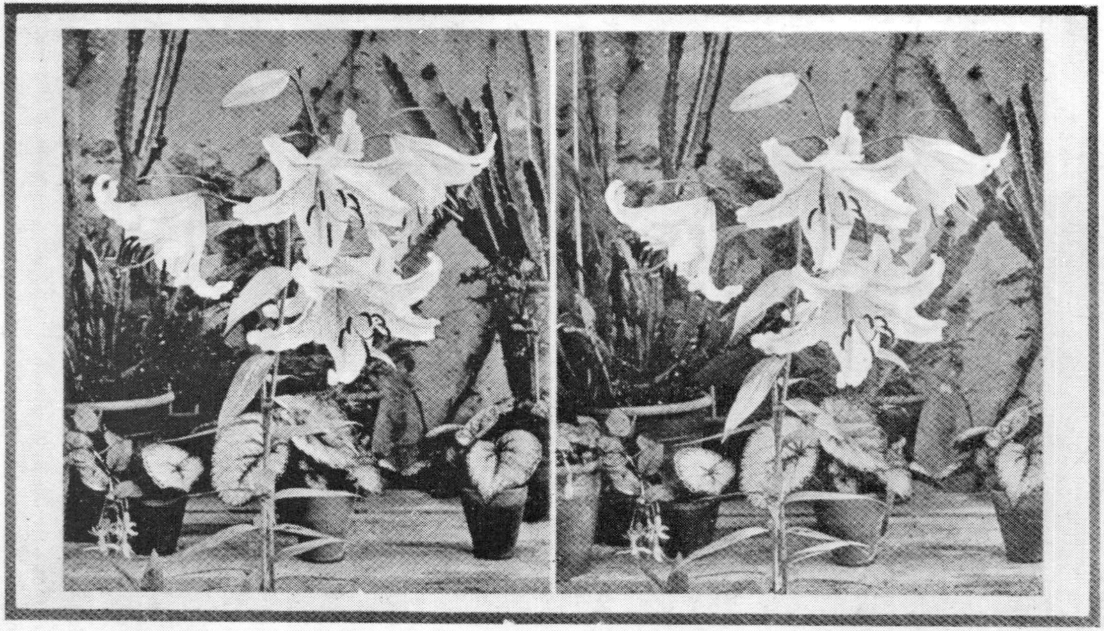

Taken by the "Exact Binocular Camera."

PLATE 3.   FIG 16 (*See page* 12).

The pointer being attached to one of the cameras and the scale plate to the other, the slightest movement of the screw, F, will be shown upon the scale plate. The position, and the degrees engraved upon the plate, are of course determined by the focal length of the lenses in use.

A stigmatic lens of 5 or 6 inches focus will be the best for general exterior work, but its depth of focus should not be very great, otherwise an artificial effect in the stereoscope will result from the dis-

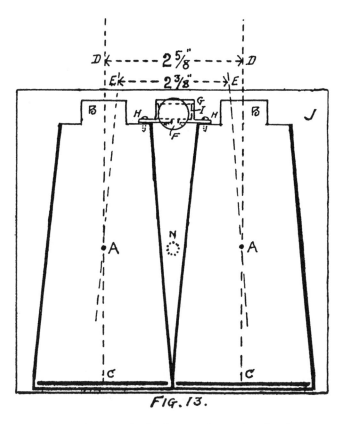

FIG. 13.

similar pair of pictures obtained. We have already shown that in Nature the images of objects at different distances from the observer cannot be projected upon the retina of the eye, equally clear at one accommodation, therefore if we use the lenses of deep focal value, we shall produce pictures rendering near and remote objects almost equal

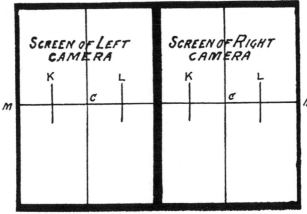

FIG. 14.

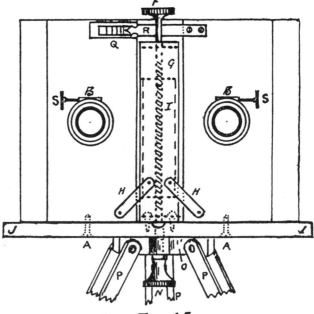

FIG. 15.

in definition, and which will destroy rather than increase a natural sensation otherwise produced.

Successive Exposures.—Although accompanied with various disadvantages, there are many ways of taking the dissimilar pair of pictures other than with a camera fitted with a pair of lenses. Fig. 17 is a board having a slot at D through which the screw of the camera passes, and is secured by a winged nut to the under side. With the

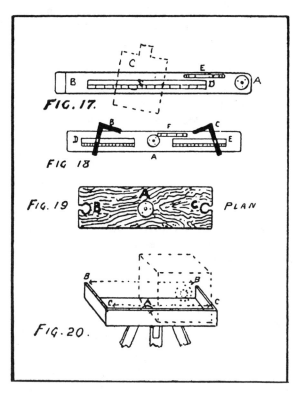

FIG. 17.

FIG 18

FIG. 19   PLAN

FIG. 20.

camera in the position indicated by the dotted lines, C, the first plate is exposed. The board carrying the camera is then turned 180 degrees on A (which is the point at which it is attached to the tripod). The camera is now turned on its own axis and directed again to the object to be photographed, when another plate is exposed. By means of a scale marked along the edge of the slot D, the proper convergence of the lens is found.

A very similar apparatus is that shown in Fig. 18, but in this case the board is not turned between the exposures, but the camera removed from the slot D to slot E, the board itself being attached to the tripod head at A. At B and C detachable squares are provided, whereby the proper position of the camera is determined.

Fig. 19 shows a simple board which is used very much in the same manner as the two just described, but it does not permit of any modification in the distance between the two points from which the pictures are taken. One exposure is made with the camera attached at B, and a second with the camera attached at C, the board itself being screwed to the tripod head at A. An apparatus termed " the stereoscopic tray " (Fig. 20) enables a hand camera to be used for stereoscopic work. The camera indicated by the dotted lines is placed at either end of the tray, an exposure made, and then the camera moved to the opposite end for the second exposure. The distance between C, C, being less than the distance between B, B, the axis of the lens in the two separate positions is made to converge upon the subject. The stereoscopic adapter (Fig. 21) is an improvement on the apparatus already mentioned, inasmuch that the work of shifting the camera between the two exposures is greatly simplified. Thus, the camera is fixed to the block B, with the lens pointing over A. One exposure having been made, B, carrying the camera with it, is moved in the direction of the arrow C till the two blocks are again touching each other, when the second plate is exposed. The parallel movement is regulated by a pair of metal links communicating with the two blocks. F is the screw and nut by which the apparatus is connected to the tripod head. A specimen of work produced by means of this instrument is given in Fig 21a, Plate 4. An apparatus similar to the above, but with the addition of adjustable means for the separation of the lenses, is shown in Fig. 22, two blocks, C, B, are connected together by four links working parallel. Two of these links are seen at E, F. A scale is provided at J, which has a projection at right angles, upon which rests the adjusting screw G. It is obvious that by turning the screw in or out, as the case may be, the play of the carrying block B will be diminished or increased, so that when G is screwed right in, the separation in the two positions of the lens will be less than it will when G is only partly screwed home. The camera employed is attached to the block B, one exposure being made with it in the two positions D and A.

Another method whereby the dissimilar pair of pictures may be

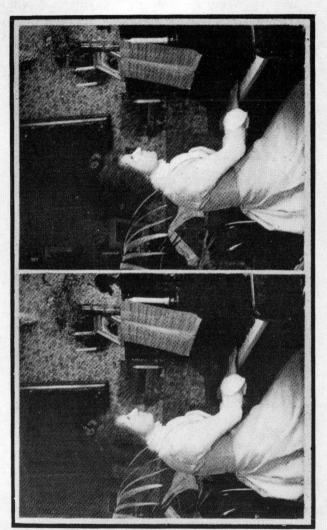

PLATE 4.   Taken with the Stereoscopic Adapter.   FIG. 21A (*See page* 16).

produced, will be shown by reference to Fig. 23. A is a half-plate camera attached to the tripod in the usual manner with a T-screw; two ordinary screws, D and E, are fixed horizontally to the tripod head in the manner shown, whilst a third screw, C, is fixed to the underside of the baseboard of the camera in such a position that as the latter is turned to the right or left, as the case may be, the screw C comes into contact with D or E at right angles.

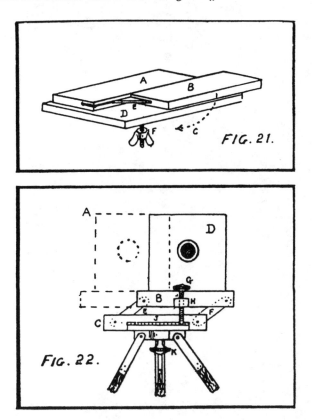

FIG. 21.

FIG. 22.

To find out the exact position on the baseboard where the second horizontal screw D should be fixed, the image on the first half of the screen with the camera in the first position (with the screws C and E touching) is noted, and the camera turned till the same image occupies exactly the same position as before, but on the second half of the screen. The screw C is then inserted in the baseboard touching the

c

screw D, when the movement of the camera is limited to the space between the horizontal screws.

To take the view so that no transposition of the prints will be necessary, and also that only one-half is taken on the plate at each exposure, an ordinary half-plate is cut in two, and one-half made opaque by exposing to light. This opaque glass is placed in the dark slide in front of the plate to be exposed. It thus covers up exactly one-half of the plate. The camera is now turned till the vertical screw touches one of the horizontal screws. The view is focused, and kept well within the limits of the half of the screen that is diagonally opposite the subject. Thus, if the camera is pointed to the left, as in the illustration, with the screw C in contact with E, the

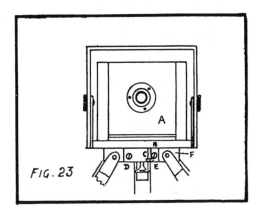

FIG. 23

subject is focused on the right of the screen, and then the dark slide is shaken so that the opaque glass falls to the bottom, when it will cover up the left-hand side of the plate. It is inserted in the camera in the usual manner, and an exposure made. It is important to note that the left view should be received on the right of the plate, otherwise transposition of the prints will be necessary.

One-half of the plate having been exposed in the manner described, the camera is turned so that the screw C comes into contact with the screw D : the dark slide is withdrawn, and the opaque glass shaken to the opposite end (covering the half just exposed). It is then replaced in the camera, and the other half exposed. The result is a stereoscopic negative that may be printed from direct, with the dissimilar pictures in their proper order for immediate examination in the stereoscope.

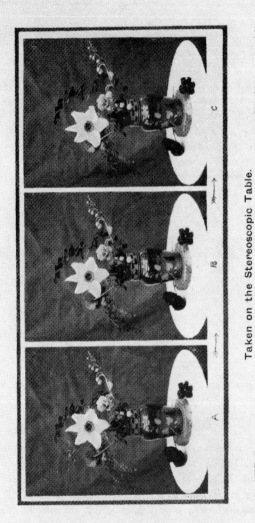

PLATE 5.

Taken on the Stereoscopic Table.   FIG. 25 (*See page* 19).

Our series would be incomplete without making brief mention of the stereoscopic table shown in Fig. 24. The edge of this circular stand is divided into 360 degrees of a complete circle. If an object, B, is placed in the centre, by turning the table five degrees between

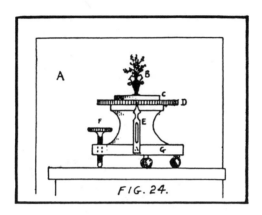

FIG. 24.

each exposure of a plate, a stereoscopic photograph of the object under every aspect will be secured. To the base is fixed an indicator, E, showing the number of degrees the table is turned. A spirit-level is also provided, and the adjustment made by means of the screw F. The background, A, is perfectly plain, and it is placed some distance from the object, so that no shadow shall fall upon it. Three successive

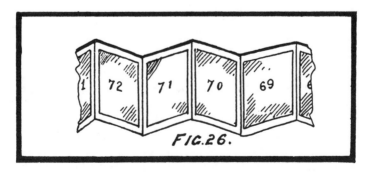

FIG.26.

pictures obtained upon the stereoscope table are shown in Fig. 25, Plate 5. Such stereograms, for convenience, are mounted on a panoramic folding mount, Fig. 26. The view passes through the stereoscope from left to right, so that C, Plate 5, passes out of view, and the picture B, which had been the left eye picture, becomes the picture for the right eye, whilst the following picture, A, is presented to the left eye, and so on till the complete set, numbering seventy-two pictures, has been examined.

Simultaneous Exposures.—We have shown that under certain conditions stereograms may be secured by a double exposure, or more correctly speaking, by the successive exposure of two plates. It is obvious, however, that this class of work can only be satisfactorily accomplished under favourable circumstances. The subject chosen must be immovable, equally lighted, and the exposures equally timed. When this double exposure system is adopted and a landscape is to form the stereogram, it is, for obvious reasons, necessary to choose a

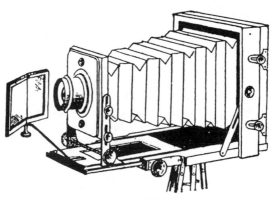

FIG. 27.

clear day, when the sky is free from clouds, or a day when the sky is completely overcast. In the first instance, the second exposure should be made as quickly after the first as it is possible, otherwise a movement in the position of the shadows will cause a very disagreeable effect when the pictures are examined in the stereoscope. The advantage claimed for the double exposure system is that it enables the amateur to use his ordinary camera, thereby securing a sensible reduction in the cost of apparatus. In recent years, however, simultaneous exposures are not confined to a stereoscopic camera. The instrument known as the "Stereoscopic Transmitter" (invented by the author 10 years ago) enables an ordinary camera to be used for stereoscopic work, whilst the dissimilar images are simultaneously received upon one plate, side by side. This instrument, attached to a

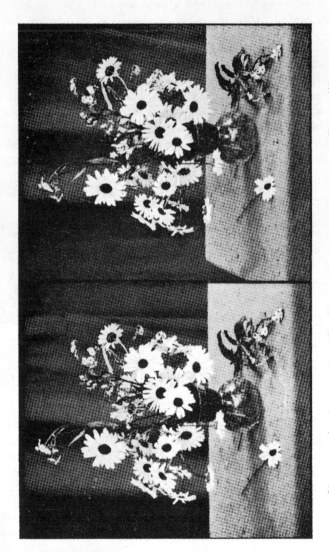

PLATE 6.   Stereoscopic phases taken simultaneously by the Stereoscopic Transmitter.

FIG. 29 (*See page* 21).

"Lancaster's half-plate Instantograph," is shown in Fig. 27, and its working will be easily understood by reference to Fig. 28. A is the ordinary single lens camera; B, the reflected twin lens camera, produced by the transmitter C, the dotted lines showing the way in which the two views are conveyed to the transmitter and from thence through the single lens to the sensitive plate. From this it will be seen that the instrument consists of a pair of plane mirrors fixed in small frames and set at a large angle to each other. Whilst the views are thus reversed they are at the same time transposed upon the plate, so that when the negative has been developed it is ready to be printed from direct, and the dissimilar pair are in their proper order for examination in the stereoscope. A specimen of work produced in a

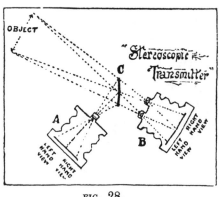

FIG. 28.

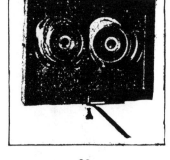

FIG. 29A.

single lens camera by using the transmitter is given in Fig. 29, Plate 6, but because this specimen happens to be of a still life subject, it should not be supposed that the instrument is confined to this class of work. On the contrary, as we have already shown, the dissimilar pictures may be taken instantaneously and simultaneously, and the subject may be a collection of moving objects. An elevation of the Transmitter is shown in Fig. 29A, and the mode of attaching it to a camera having no projecting baseboard is shown in Fig. 29B. It is a fact of some interest that, as the images on the ground glass screen of the camera are in their proper order for the stereoscope when projected thereon by the Transmitter; the stereoscopic relief may be inspected by using either an ordinary pair of refracting prisms or the

Pocket Stereoscope described in another part under Section II., "Stereoscopes."

Another instrument, also invented by the author in the year 1894, whereby the dissimilar pictures are obtained with an ordinary camera at one exposure, is shown in Fig. 30. Here the "Stereophotoduplicon" is seen complete with its shutter attached. When used complete it is placed on the lens mount as shown in Fig. 31, after the manner of a shutter. If, on the other hand, it is used without the shutter, it is simply attached to the front of the camera as shown in Fig. 32. By reference to Fig. 33, the principle on which this instru-

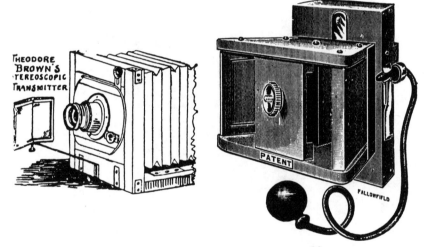

FIG. 29B. FIG. 30.

ment is based will be readily understood. Suppose the object to be photographed to be situated at E, E, the camera at D, and the lens at C. By means of reflection two views of the object are carried to the plate in the camera thus, by reflection from the mirrors A, A, to B, B, and from thence through the lens to the plate. It may be supposed that as the images are reflected before reaching the sensitive plate that considerable amount of light is lost, but such is not the case, and the operator will find that there is no perceivable difference of exposure required when taking an ordinary view direct, or a stereoscopic pair with the apparatus attached. The example given in Fig. 34A, Plate 7, was taken on an ordinary Ilford plate, with a single

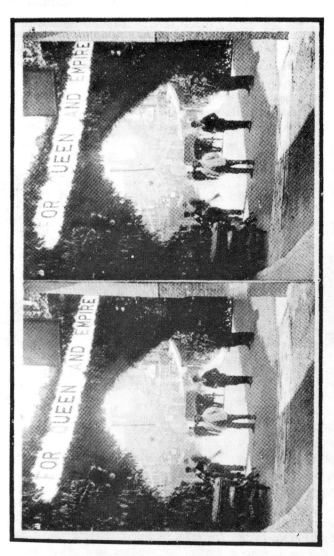

Instantaneous Picture taken with an ordinary single lens camera and the Stereo-photo-duplicon.

FIG. 34A (*See page* 22).

PLATE 7.

view lens working at F/25 in one twentieth second. It is obvious from this result that little light has been lost by reflection. With this instrument it is unnecessary to transpose the prints, as this is effected by the mirrors before the images reach the sensitive plate. In Figs. 34, 35, 36 and 37 we give diagrams showing how similar arrangements or combinations of mirrors and prisms may be adjusted for stereoscopy with a single lens. Fig. 34 consists of two mirrors, A, B, and a pair of total reflecting prisms, C, D. Fig. 35 is very similar, the only difference being that the prisms are used outside instead of at the centre. Fig. 36 consists of four prisms, whilst Fig. 37 is composed of a single prism with two surfaces on the front slightly inclined, as shown in the diagram.

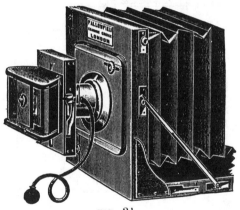

FIG. 31.

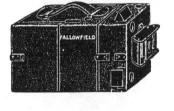

FIG. 32.

The four methods just described are not so good as that embodied under the name of the stereophotoduplicon; first, because prisms are more troublesome to adjust than mirrors, and are also more expensive, and secondly (referring especially to Fig. 37), the separation between the two points, A, B, is not sufficient to give a full stereoscopic relief.

Before closing the subject of simultaneous exposures we might mention the stereoscopic attachment shown in Fig. 38. This apparatus makes it possible to secure very satisfactory stereographs with a pair of ordinary No. 1 Nipper cameras. The cameras are placed one on each side of the centre partition, and fixed there by means of the turn-catch which fits on the view-finder screws and the extra turn-button at the back. By means of the shaft pivoted to the twin levers shown in the front, the shutters are actuated simultaneously. The partition is thicker at the back than at the front, being somewhat the form of a wedge, so that whilst the cameras are held close to the sides of the partition, the axes of the lenses are slightly inclined. The effect of this is that the whole of the plate in each camera is utilised, which

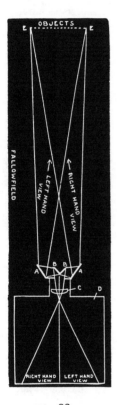

FIG. 33.

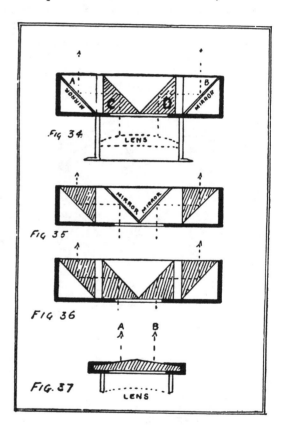

would not be the case were their axes parallel, as we shall further explain presently.

Fig. 39, Plate 8, was taken with this twin "Nipper" stereoscopic attachment. On examining this specimen in an ordinary stereoscope, it will be seen that the subject appears to lie at a plane beyond the margin of the combined picture; an effect that should always be aimed

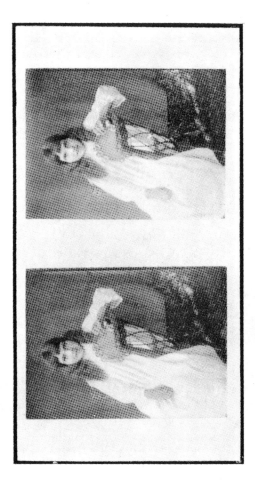

PLATE 8. Taken with two "Nipper Cameras" and the Stereoscopic Attachment.

FIG. 39 (*See page* 24).

at when masking or trimming stereoscopic pictures. That this effect is the most natural, and therefore the most desirable, will be understood by reference to Fig. 40. Let E, H, be a wall, with an opening (door or window) at F, G. If the observer stands with his eyes in the position of L and R, on looking through the opening to the view beyond there will be objects within the space A, B, F, visible only to the right eye, R ; and objects in the space C, D, G, visible only to the left eye, L. Now, although such objects are not binocularly observed, they are, nevertheless, essential to the combined effect of the dissimilar compositions.

The left eye print will include all objects within F, B, D, G, and the right eye print all objects within F, A, C, G, and, whether masked or

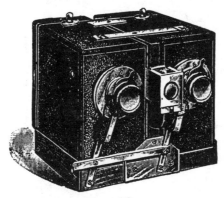

FIG. 38.

trimmed, under such conditions the combined images will appear to lie beyond the plane F, G, as they always should. If we look again at Fig. 39, we shall find that these conditions are fulfilled with the desired result already mentioned.

Errors and Defects.—Having considered the various appliances by which the stereograph may be secured, let us look at some of the errors made by the inexperienced operator. When we remember that many of the binocular cameras still manufactured and supplied for stereoscopic work lack the means whereby the lenses may be adjusted for near and distant objects, it is not surprising to find amateur stereoscopists falling into various errors respecting the trimming and masking of their prints. With all the improvements of the modern day camera there is abundant evidence that some manufacturers need yet to learn the principle on which a stereoscopic camera should be based, in order to secure the most satisfactory results in the stereoscope.

Since, however, thousands of cameras more or less defective in principle are now in the hands of operators, it may prove of interest to suggest remedies whereby prints from negatives obtained in faulty cameras may be corrected.

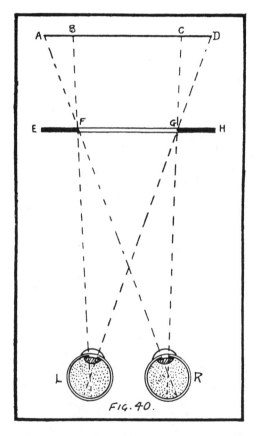

FIG. 40.

It is quite recently we came across a whole collection of views, evidently the fruits from the same camera, for the following disagreeable effect presented itself on every slide ; there was present at each end of the slide a portion of view, as at B and C, Fig. 42, Plate 9, altogether superfluous to the combined image in the stereoscope.

Perhaps it would be more correct to say portions of the print which

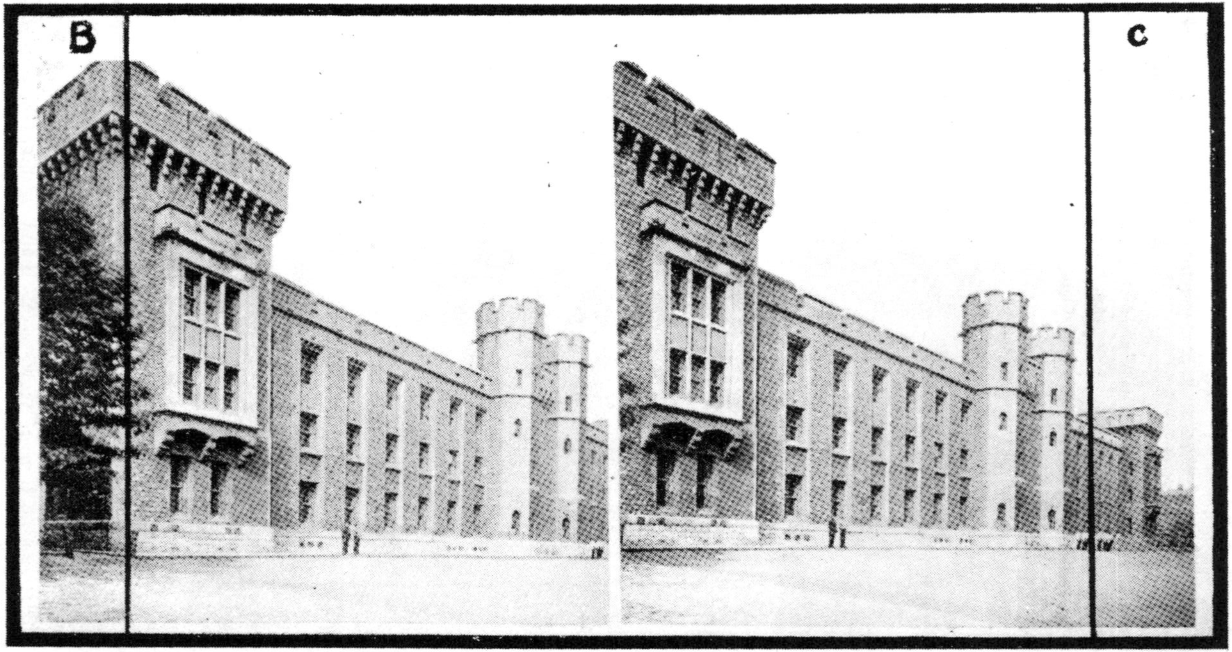

B

C

FIG 42 (*See page 26*).

PLATE 9.

should have been occupied by objects not present were filled up with portions of the landscape which should have been excluded. These views were obtained in a camera not only lacking all the means of varying the separation of the two lenses, but also with the lenses with their axes parallel, as shown in diagram, Fig. 41.

The reader will, of course, understand that the accompanying diagram exaggerates these conditions. Suppose the view to be taken

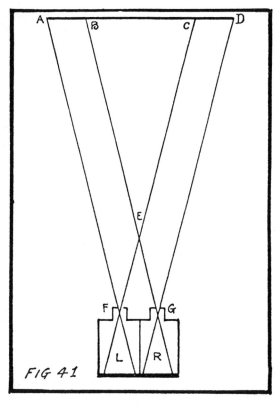

FIG 41

to lie between A and D, the left lens F will take in a portion A, B not taken in by the right lens G, whilst the right lens will cover a portion C, D, not taken in by the left lens F. It is obvious, therefore, with such a construction, prints from the negatives, after being transposed in the usual way, have on the outer edge of each pair a strip of view absolutely unnecessary, whilst a portion that should have been there is missing.

In the present instance the operator must be content with views a little narrower than the standard size, for although a sacrifice is made by cutting away the superfluous portions, the disagreeable effect otherwise produced is prevented.

A stereoscopic view may be good from a technical standpoint, and well selected artistically, and yet contain certain peculiarities detrimental to the best effect in the stereoscope.

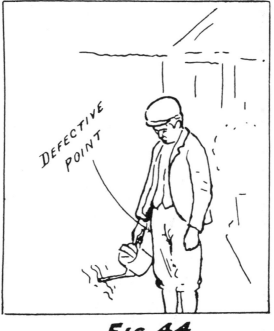

FIG. 44.

When examining the dissimilar photographs in this instrument, the changes which the eyes are called upon to make in order to see the combined images perfectly, are not identical with those changes made when the original objects in nature are binocularly observed. There is, of course, very little difference in axial direction, but we must not forget that, for reasons already explained, there is absolutely no focusing or accommodation of the eye needed once the proper distance for the view has been determined. To this fact may be traced the cause of many of the phenomena peculiar to stereoscopic work.

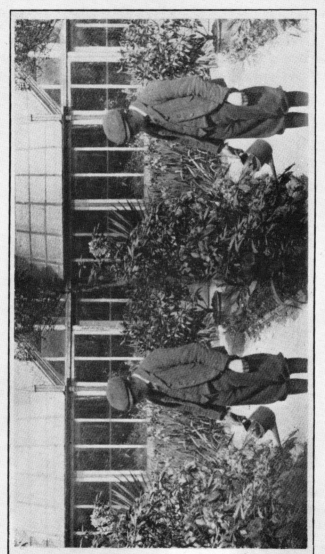

PLATE 10.

A Defective Stereogram.

FIG. 48 (*See page 29*).

If the successful production of stereoscopic photographs is a task more difficult than that of making a single picture, it is because in the former case we have two distinct compositions to deal with instead of only one. One of the commonest defects that often mars the finished pictures is that of objects seemingly springing from their proper planes and occupying a position apparently in mid-air; we have an

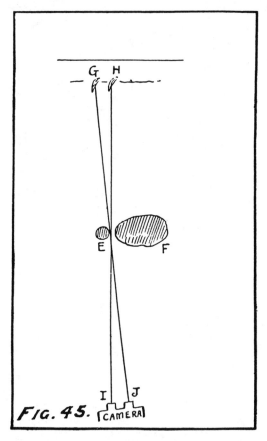

FIG. 45. CAMERA

instance of this shown in Fig. 43, Plate 10. If we examine this specimen in an ordinary stereoscope the illusion just mentioned is apparent. Between the hand holding the waterpot and the boy's leg (pointed out by the arrow in Fig. 44) an object not belonging to the figure appears. This is really a combined image of two distinct objects situated at a remote plane. Reference being made to Fig. 45, let E represent the boy's hand and F his body. When this subject was taken the lenses of the camera must have been at I and J. Two leaves, very similar in form to each other and overhanging the garden edging at G and H, were each embraced only by one lens of the camera. Thus J photographed G, whilst I photographed H. At the same time G was rendered invisible at point I by the interposition of E, likewise H was invisible at J because F intercepted. The stereoscopic result is shown in Fig. 43. Referring again to Fig. 45, the reason that G and H appear as one object and at a point between E and F, is that when the boy is being more particularly noticed the axes of the eyes meet at that plane; and as the eyes sweep over the surface no axial change is necessary for the mind to appreciate G and H as one object situated at the same distance. We have mentioned this class of error in stereoscopic work not merely to show what to avoid in a composition, but also that the reader may understand wherein natural binocular vision differs from the viewing of a stereogram in a stereoscope.

This illusion would not present itself in nature, though the eyes may be situated at I and J (Fig. 45), for whilst the eyes of the observer were accommodated for the distance at which the boy stood, objects so far off as G and H would be out of focus upon the retina, and thus partially rendered invisible; a provision of nature difficult to imitate.

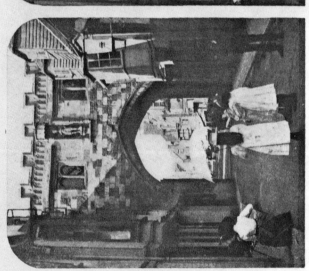

PLATE 11

High Street, Close Gate, Salisbury.

(*See page* 90).

PART II.

STEREOSCOPES.

Stereoscopes.—As anyone may find on investigation, long before the invention of the stereoscope philosophers had noted the dissimilarity of the images projected upon the retina of the eyes in binocular vision; and it is more than probable that the dissimilar diagrams which they constructed were sometimes examined coalesced, by a divergence or crossing of the axes, which would obviously result in stereoscopic relief. Be this as it may, it was not until the year

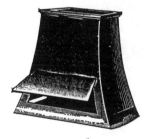

FIG. 1.

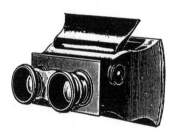

FIG. 2

1834, at the suggestion of Mr. Elliot, that means of aiding the eyes in the observation was made. Following this in the year 1838, Wheatstone constructed his reflecting instrument, the principle of which is well known. Brewster, observing the defects of this apparatus, invented the Lenticular Stereoscope, to which he afterwards added various improvements, making the apparatus in a vast number of different shapes and forms to meet both commercial and scientific requirements. It is not the purpose of this book to give an exhaustive treatise on the works of this eminent philosopher, as particulars of his interesting conceptions and admirable labours may be found in other publications. It will suffice to make brief reference to the first instruments and then to pass on to mention some of the modern patterns, including those which, although without great commercial value, perhaps, are nevertheless interesting from a scientific standpoint.

Box Stereoscope.—Brewster's early stereoscopes were generally made in box form, as shown in Fig. 1. To this pattern were added frames in which the lenses were fitted to sliding mounts, for focusing purposes as well as for adjustment as regards separation. Fig. 2 shows a pattern in which rack-work focusing adjustment is effected by means of a milled thumbscrew extended through the side. To increase the capacity of the instrument it is sometimes made in column form, Fig. 3, and this design has been elaborated in a variety of ways,

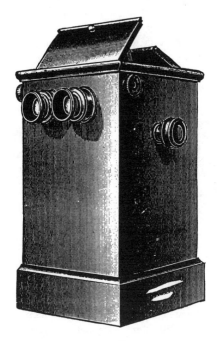

FIG. 3.

and is sometimes much taller than the illustration and styled the "Saloon" stereoscope. In some of the best instruments provision is made to prevent distortion and chromatic fringes, these defects being overcome by using chromatic eyepieces. Oliver Wendall Holmes, who has done much to further the interests of stereoscopy, designed the instrument shown in Fig. 4, a pattern which from commercial and efficient standpoints has proved a great success.

Baird's Lothian Stereoscope.—Shown in the two accompanying figures, 5 and 6, and is composed of gun metal and brass, with lenses of considerable magnifying power and about 4-inch focal length. The handle is detachable. Just above the handle and between the lens

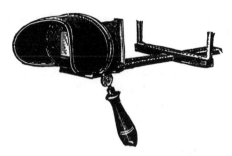

FIG. 4.

mounts there is a crossbar attached, which causes the variation in separation of the lenses to be altered simultaneously, when one or the other is moved by the hand in the manner shown in Fig. 6. By such provision the instrument is rendered suitable for any person, whatever may be the distance between the pupillary centres. The proper distance for the slide in relation to the lenses is arrived at by sliding the

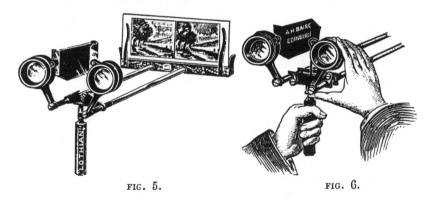

FIG. 5.   FIG. 6.

view holder along the carrying tubes, the latter being detachable so that the instrument may be used for the examination of stereoscopic prints mounted in albums. The admirable and, we may add, service-able characteristics of the Lothian will be appreciated by the serious

D

stereoscopic worker, though it may not be so popular with the general public as the simpler form of stereoscopes are destined to be.

Tylar's " Best Portable Stereoscope."—Shown in Figs. 7 and 8. This instrument is exceedingly portable. The lenses are mounted on a cloth covered board, which is detachable, so that it can be packed inside the body of the instrument, as shown in Fig. 8. Its length is $7\frac{1}{8}$ inches, width 4 inches, thickness $\frac{1}{2}$ inch, weight 4 ounces, and range of focus 9 inches.

Biloscope.—This is the name given to a small portable stereoscope, Fig. 9, issued by the enterprising firm of " Bile Beans Manufacturing Company." It is of the cloth covered cardboard type, fitted with lenses of $3\frac{1}{4}$-inch focal length. The sets of miniature stereographs sent out with this collapsible instrument are beautifully printed, and would bear inspection through far more powerful magnifiers than those used.

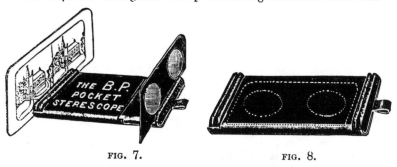

FIG. 7.   FIG. 8.

The same instrument is being imported from Germany under another name, whilst the Rotary Photographic Company are issuing a similar instrument in metal which they call the " Rotoscope."

Kaleidoscopic Stereoscope.—If two mirrors are fixed into frames, hinged together in book form, but whose opening is limited to an angle of 100 degrees, a stereoscope of the reflecting class will be formed. The mirrors so framed are stood on their edges in a perpendicular position, whilst the stereoscopic slide to be examined is placed about 6 inches distance from the junction of the mirrors, and facing the latter. The observer now looks over the back of the slide, and views by reflection the combined images, which appear to be situated a little behind the frames, and present the usual solidity. For further particulars see illustrated article in " The Optician and Photographic Trades Review," for April 13th, 1899.

The Reflectascope.—This is a name given to another stereoscope of the reflecting type, shown in the accompanying cut, Fig. 10. Like as with the preceding instrument the slide is examined by looking over the mount from the back and directing the eyes to a pair of mirrors. In this case, however, the face of the mirrors are turned slightly away from each other, the resultant image appearing to occupy a position behind them. The best results are obtained by allowing a strong light to fall upon the slide whilst the mirrors are kept in the shade. This instrument is very compact as it folds flat, occupying no more room than about a dozen stereoscopic photographs. It is also worthy of note that, as the combined image appears about 12 inches distant from the observer's eyes, no abnormal strain is experienced when the

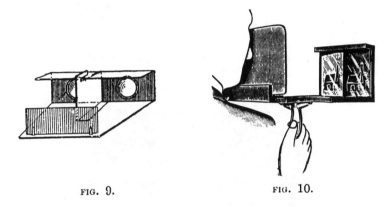

FIG. 9. FIG. 10.

axes are converged upon the view, and as the results are obtained by reflection no focal adjustments are necessary.

Pocket Stereoscope.—Fig. 11. This instrument was designed by the author in the year 1895, its construction is such that the right eye looking through the scope sees a reflection of the right hand view, not at the point it actually occupies but superimposed upon its companion element. If a stereoscopic slide is looked at without any instrument whatever, both eyes will naturally turn their axes to one point, so that only one of the stereoscopic elements are viewed, and no relief results. When the Pocket Stereoscope is brought into use, whilst the eyes are still permitted to look in their natural direction, each eye will see a different view over the same point, *i.e..* the right eye will see the right element of the stereoscopic slide by reflection, whilst the left eye will see the left element direct, and combined with the right, resulting in the desired stereoscopic effect. The mode of

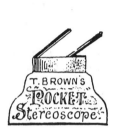

FIG. 11.

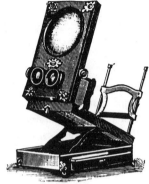

FIG. 13.

using this stereoscope is shown in Fig. 12. As indicated in this cut, a pile of views can be looked through with great rapidity. Views mounted in albums may also be examined stereoscopically, whilst the

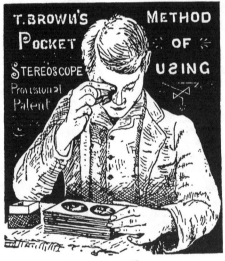

FIG. 12.

smallness of the instrument, 1¾ inches square, makes it the most portable appliance of practical utility.

It should also be noticed that stereoscopic transparencies projected upon the Optical Magic Lantern Screen, side by side, forming what may be termed enlarged Stereoscopic Views, may be inspected with the Pocket Stereoscope, and seen in bold relief.

Stereographoscope.—Fig. 13 shows an instrument suitable for the drawing-room table. In addition to the stereoscopic eyepieces, it is also furnished with a larger lens for the inspection of ordinary photographs.

Complementary Stereoscope.—This instrument, invented by the author and fully described in the " British Journal of Photography " for November 2nd, 1900, is an apparatus for the alternate examination of a positive and negative transparent picture, the one being dissimilar to the other. Provision is made whereby the axes of the eyes, whilst allowed to converge in a natural manner, meet at a point, first occupied by the negative and then by the positive, thus :—After stimulating the right eye with light sifted through the negative image, the movable partition is suddenly made to intercept the view in such a manner as to give the stimulated eye an opportunity of seeing the complementary image, which, of course, would be a positive. By this sudden change in the mechanism of the apparatus a dissimilar positive is presented to the left eye ; and in virtue of the fact that the recurring or complementary positive still persists upon the right retina, a stereoscopic image is visible to the observer. In place of the plain transparencies coloured ones may be used, and in some cases this would be found to make the phenomenon more apparent.

Shutter Stereoscope.—It is the natural tendency of the eyes to cross their axes at that point and plane where the object of attention happens to be situated, which makes necessary the displacement of the two pictures in the stereoscope.

As is well known, such an apparent movement of the actual picture may be effected either by a refracting or a reflecting medium, and on such principles the most practical instruments have been constructed.

Now we do not suggest that the possession of what has been termed stereoscopic vision, dispenses altogether with the necessity of resorting to such instruments for general use, but it will be acknowledged by all who have acquired this muscular control of the eyes, that being able to coalesce the images in such a manner is not merely a source of pleasure but also a serviceable attainment.

Hence, for the benefit of those who have as yet failed in the art of stereoscopic perception, I will venture to offer some assistance in the form of a shutter stereoscope.

Reference being made to the diagrams, Figs. 1 and 2, it will be seen that the apparatus contains neither prisms nor mirrors, but that this invention belongs to that class of instrument known as direct stereoscopes.

It consists of a box, of dimensions indicated, pierced with four holes

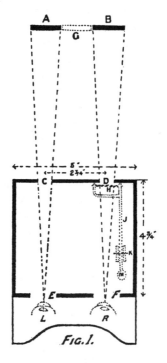

FIG. 1.

as shown at C, D, E, and F. The most essential part of this instrument is a contrivance for shutting off the light at D, when desired, and the mechanism of this being shown in both figures it will take but few words to make clear its construction.

J is a galvanised iron rod, to which is pivoted the shutter H. The iron rod turns on a pivot at K, and is actuated by pressing the knob M, projecting through the top of the box.

The interior of the box is blackened to prevent possible side reflections, a hood and handle is fitted to the exterior of the box as shown, and the shutter stereoscope is complete. Now how is this stereoscope used, and why does it assist in the art of the stereoscopic perception?

An ordinary stereoscopic slide is place on a table about two feet from the observer. The stereoscope, with the shutter H closed as in Fig. 2, is held to the face exactly in the same manner as an ordinary pattern stereoscope. The view to be examined, supposed to be at A and B, Fig. 1, is so placed that the left eye L sees the left picture A through the opening C.

It is apparent that by reason of the shutter H the right eye R is prevented from seeing anything, until the shutter be raised by pressing

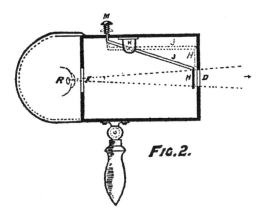

FIG.2.

the knob M, when to the surprise of the observer he sees not two separate pictures, as when looking at the view without the stereoscope, but apparently one image in bold relief.

The reason of this result is found in the effects produced upon the right eye R by the shutter, in preventing the light emanating from the view reaching it.

Thus, under such circumstances the iris of the right eye will be considerably dilated, the crystalline lens flattened, whilst the plane in focus upon its retina will be considerably farther back than that at which the stereoscopic slide is situated.

Hence, as the shutter H is raised, the eye involuntarily accommodates itself upon the distant plane, to the distance where the stereoscopic view is placed, with the desired result of a combined image in the mind of the observer.

Till the operator has become acquainted with the instrument, he may find it necessary to look for some time with the left eye only, so that the attention may be fixed by muscular control.

I have no doubt that after using this instrument a few times, the operator will find to his great pleasure he has acquired the power of stereoscopic vision.

Lensless Stereoscope for Small Transparencies.—The natural tendency of the eyes to turn their axes to one point necessitates the interposition of some refracting medium in order that the stereoscopic view may be properly observed. If, however, the dissimilar pair of pictures be reduced in size as regards the separation of corresponding points in the views, it is possible to place them so that they may be seen whilst the eyes are still in a position with their axes converged, dispensing entirely with lenses for the purpose of refracting the rays.

In order that this may be successfully accomplished, the eyes, however, require some assistance, so that accommodation may be effected without change in the direction of the axes. The instrument here described has been designed to accomplish this, and it will be found useful in the examination of small stereoscopic transparencies, specially made to the size of the lantern slide.

Fig. 1 represents a sectional view. The lensless stereoscope consists of a frame-work in the form of a box with a hood. G is a piece of ground glass fixed in the back of this frame work. E and F are two grooved blocks forming a holder in which the transparencies are slipped. The transparency, which contains the dissimilar pair of views, is of the same size as an ordinary lantern slide.

C and D indicate the two dissimilar views. The black portions at the end of the slide represent the binding strips. J is a screen which prevents the left eye L, looking through the opening H, from seeing anything but the left hand view C ; and the right eye R, looking through the opening I, from seeing anything but the right hand view D.

The stereoscope is used in the following manner. The transparency is dropped into the grooves E and F. The instrument is then held up to the light, and the eyes of the observer, placed at the openings H and I, are directed to the ground-glass screen at a point some distance higher than the top of the transparency, the latter will then be seen

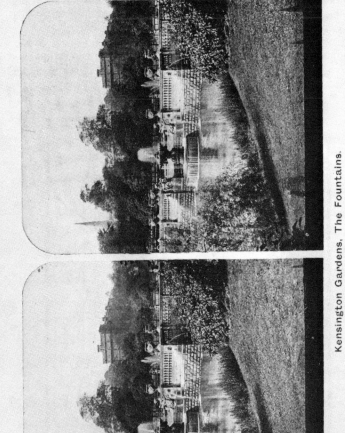

PLATE 12.

Kensington Gardens, The Fountains.

(See page 90).

stereoscopically at a plane A B, for as the eyes are gradually lowered until they look through the centres of the respective pictures, accommodation instinctively takes place and the stereoscopic relief will thus have been obtained without any undue strain caused by attempting to look parallel.

Pinhole Stereoscope.—If we place the eye any closer than four inches to a sheet of printed matter, such as this page, we shall find that the wording is too indistinct to be read. But on interposing a

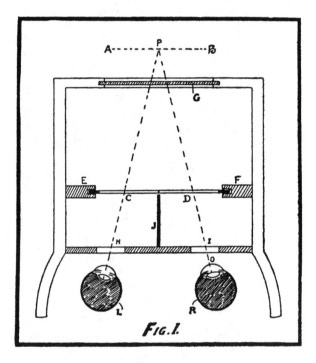

Fig. I.

piece of card or paper pierced with a pinhole between the eye and the letterpress, we shall find that, although the eye is as close as ever, we are able to read this matter, and to see it clearly. But not only do we see this lettering distinctly, but every letter has become enlarged. This is fully realised by examining the small E in Fig. 1 (next page). We find that the small E, on being observed in the manner described, becomes equal in size to the large one on the right of it. Further, we notice that not only has it become enlarged, but the rays emanating

therefrom are refracted from the left to the right, *i.e.*, when viewing it
with the left eye. On viewing it with the right eye, the rays will be
refracted towards the left. We shall understand this change in magnitude and definition by reference to Figs. 2 and 3. Let A in each
case be the plane at which the reading matter is placed. Looking at
it with one eye, and without the pierced cardboard, the conditions will
be as shown in Fig. 2. The lettering will be seen indistinctly, because

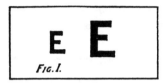

the rays are brought to a focus too soon, so that the distinct image is
at B, instead of on the retina at E.

Now, if we interpose the cardboard D, Fig. 3, and look through the
hole C, the letterpress is seen distinctly, because the focus of the rays
is delayed, being brought back upon the retina E. In other words, D
forms an artificial iris, so that only a small centre portion of the crystalline lens is employed.

This threefold change of definition—magnitude—and direction of rays, may be adapted for stereoscopic observation, and it

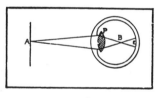 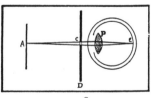

FIG. 2.   FIG. 3.

is upon the basis of these facts we construct the pinhole stereoscope.

Fig. 4 shows a plan of the apparatus; the dissimilar views F and
G, consisting of small transparencies, are backed up with a piece of
ground-glass K fitted into the framework. The size of the views does
not exceed one square inch, and they have a separation of about one
and a half inches between their centres.

A pair of stops, H and I, acting, as I have already intimated, as artificial irises, are placed just in front of the two openings, M and N, made in the front of the instrument. It is through these openings the observer looks, with the eyes situated at L and R. A screen, J, prevents more than one view being seen with either eye at the same time. The dissimilar pictures will appear to coalesce at some plane situated behind the instrument, but in reality they are very near the eyes. Q is the hood of the apparatus, so shaped to fit the face closely, and thus exclude superfluous light.

In Fig. 5 we have an interior view, showing the mechanism for varying the separation of the stops H and I, so that the same instru-

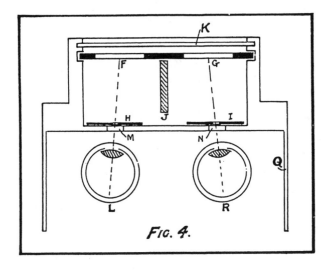

FIG. 4.

ment may be used by persons whose eyes vary in degree of separation and power of refraction.

The two stops lie close to the inside surface of the front of this instrument, and are kept in place by being fitted into grooved plates 5 and 6. At the centre, and in a vertical position, a spindle, V, turns in the plate W and 7. A thread is worked on the centre portion of this spindle, which works in a corresponding thread made in the block U, which is then connected to the stop plates H and I by the links X and Y.

It is obvious that if the knob S is turned from left to right, the thread on the spindle will cause the block U to rise, so that the links X and Y will simultaneously draw the stop plates closer together. If, on the other hand, the knob is turned in the opposite direction, the block U will drop, at the same time spreading the links X and Y, which in turn will cause the stop plates to increase their separation. To complete the instrument the usual foldable handle Z is attached by means of screws to the under side.

As the views under observation are situated much nearer to the face than they are in the ordinary American pattern stereoscope, the instrument may be packed in a very small space, and the transparencies likewise are very compact.

By introducing some modifications in the design of this instrument,

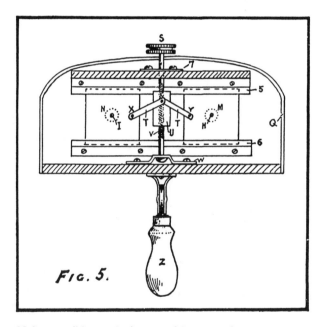

FIG. 5.

it would be possible to fit it up with a continuous roll of views, printed on films, and as the outside width over all need not exceed three inches, the instrument is one admirably suited for the purpose.

Revolving Microscopic Stereoscope.—The construction of this instrument is clearly shown in Fig. 1. It consists of a pair of circular frames B, B, fitted with concave discs, blackened on the inside, and pierced with a hole in the centre, the position of which is shown by the dotted circles.

In front of each of these discs a view carrier, C, is pivoted at its centre to the lower portion of the discs in such a position that the microscopic views contained in the cones 1 to 6 pass successively across the openings in the disc through which they are viewed.

Before going any further with the description of its construction it may be as well to say what kind of microscopic photographs are used in the instrument. Every reader is doubtless familiar with the minute

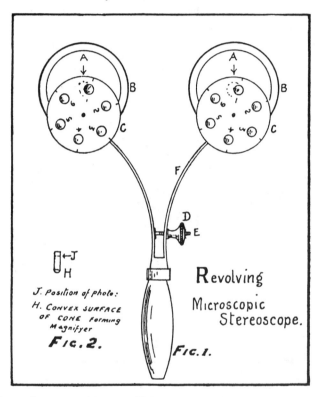

J. Position of photo:
H. Convex surface of cone forming magnifier

Fig. 2.

Revolving
Microscopic
Stereoscope.

Fig. 1.

photographs mounted in magnifying cones, and fitted into small articles, such as may be purchased at a stationer's shop. I refer to the microscopic photographs fitted into pen-holders, pocket knives, and other fancy articles.

In these we may generally expect to find six distinct views of the locality in which we have made our purchase, and it is really surprising how distinctly even the small details of the views are seen in these cheap magnifiers. The views employed in this microscopic stereoscope are similar to these, but should be of better quality. Instead of crowding six distinct views into one small cone I use slightly larger cones and mount only one view in each (Fig. 2).

The magnifying cones in the carrier revolving on the left-eye disc contain views taken from the left-eye standpoint, and the magnifying cones in the carrier revolving on the right-eye disc contain views taken from the right-eye standpoint. In other words, the two revolving carriers each contain a set of six views, dissimilar to those contained in its companion carrier, so that on being coalesced they produce stereoscopic relief. The instrument shown in Fig. 1 illustrates the arrangement for a set of six pairs.

As the corresponding views in the two carriers are brought opposite the openings in the concave discs, the observer sees a magnified image

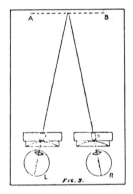

of each, apparently a few inches away from the face, where they are blended together, and produce the desired results.

The position in which the cones are mounted is shown in Fig. 3. It will be seen by reference to this diagram that the cones C, D, are turned inwards, so that the axes of the eyes L and R come exactly in a line with the axes of the cones. The effect of this adjustment is that, whilst the photographs are really within the cones C and D, they appear to the observer to be situated at A, B, coalesced, and producing stereoscopic relief.

The two circular frames B, B, are connected together by the steel fork F, which is adjustable by turning the thumbscrew D (Fig. 1), working on a thread made on E, which is fixed to the opposite side of the fork. This adjustment enables the same instrument to be used by different persons whose eyes may vary in degree of separation. The steel fork is securely fastened to a suitable handle, and the instrument is complete.

It is obvious that the principle on which this instrument is based permits a modification in pattern. It might be constructed to take a much larger number of views in each carrier, and the latter could be made detachable from the eyepieces, so that an unlimited number of views might be examined in the same instrument.

I have also designed a stereoscope in the form of an ordinary pair of spectacles. In this case the stereoscopic portion of the apparatus is attached to the frames usually occupied by the spectacle lenses, further and illustrated particulars of which will be found in " The English Mechanic and World of Science " for June 15th, 1900.

Pencil Stereoscope.—The same sort of microscopic view cones, as mentioned above, are used in this instrument, three pair of the dissimilar photographs being attached to the pencil case in the manner

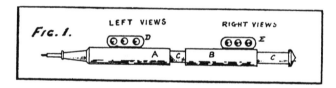

indicated in Fig. 1. The magnifying cones containing the pictures for the left eye are shown at D, whilst those for the right eye are shown at E.

Fig. 2 is a sectional diagram showing the position of the two sets of cones. The three on the left hand side are inclined to the other three on the right hand side, so that the axes of the eyes fall exactly in a line with the axes of the cones through which they are looking. The result of this arrangement is that whilst the photographs are really within the cones they appear to the observer to be situated at A', B', Fig. 2, coalesced and producing stereoscopic relief; and the images received upon the retina of the eyes have a magnitude equal to pictures observed in the ordinary prismatic instruments of larger dimensions.

It is obvious from Fig. 2 that either pair of cones may be looked through by allowing them to pass in succession before the two eyes.

In order that the same pencil stereoscope may be used by different persons whose eyes vary in degrees of separation, the portion B, carrying the right hand set of views, is made to slide along C, so that any adjustment may be secured.

Opera-Glass Stereoscope.—There are two distinct ways in which a pair of ordinary field or opera-glasses may be used as a stereoscope ; and for the examination of stereograms mounted in albums or printed in books, these instruments will be found very handy.

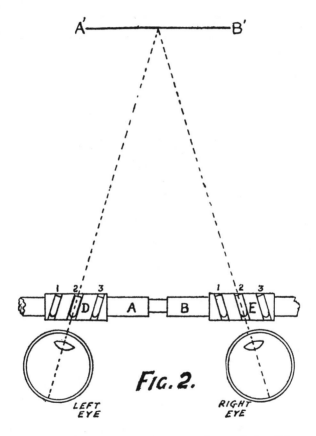

FIG. 2.

One way in which the opera-glasses may be used for this purpose is shown in the diagram, Fig. 1. It will be noticed that the instru· ment is turned the opposite way to that in which it is used for viewing distance scenes in the ordinary way. The stereoscopic views to be examined should be situated a few inches from the positive lenses.

In this way the observer will see a reduced pair of pictures apparently at the same place with the result of a solid or combined image presenting stereoscopic relief.

A still better result will be obtained by removing the negative lenses altogether and examining the dissimilar views by looking

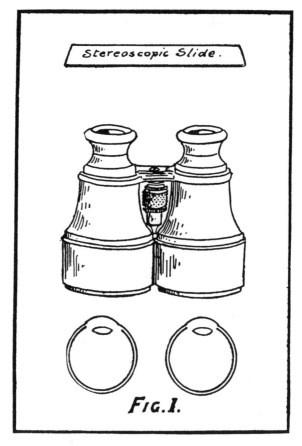

Stereoscopic Slide.

FIG. 1.

through the tubes in the ordinary way, using only the positive lenses as in Fig. 2. The result of this method will be a magnified solid image, the refraction necessary to aid the eye in coalescing the views being done by the two inner halves of the lenses.

On account of its cheapness perhaps the most popular stereoscope is that of the American pattern, but, unfortunately, though these instruments are both simple in construction and eminently effectual, by reason of the projecting portion at the back serving as a guide for the view holder, they cannot be used for the examination of stereo-

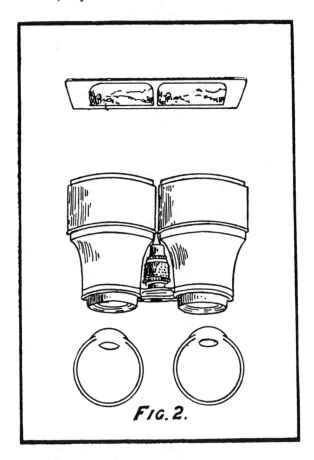

FIG. 2.

grams printed in books. Hence, as a pair of opera or field-glasses are to be found in most homes, the hint I have ventured to offer for their application to stereoscopic observation may prove of service.

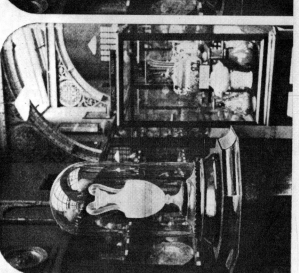

PLATE 13.

Interior, Birmingham Art Gallery.

(See page 90).

PART III.

BINOCULAR PHENOMENA AND DEMONSTRATING INSTRUMENTS.

A Stereoscopic Method of Demonstrating the Illusion of Size.
—Mental calculations, through the visual organs, are subject to a great variety of illusions, and cannot be depended upon for absolute correctness.

In estimating the size of a given object, we generally resort to methods of comparison.

Our previous experience and education in the dimensions of things doubtless helps us largely to form a fairly accurate idea, but there is

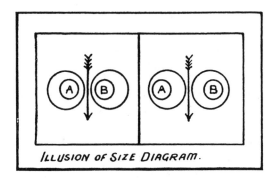

ILLUSION OF SIZE DIAGRAM.

always an uncertainty of correctness because there is always a possibility of illusion.

A man short of stature will appear to be even shorter than he really is, whilst he walks by the side of a very tall person. In colour—the artist can create various sensations in the mind of the observer by introducing degrees of contrast in his picture. In short, there are a number of ways in which the mind may be so acted upon that it becomes quite incapable of accurately estimating the exact nature and dimensions of visible objects.

That the mind is subject particularly to the illusion of size may be clearly shown thus:—Place the accompanying diagram in an ordinary stereoscope, adjusting the view carrier so that the two arrows are superimposed. It will be seen at once that, on the left hand side of the arrow, the small circle A appears nearer to the eyes than the larger one does, whilst on the right hand side of the arrow the small circle B appears behind the larger one. It will thus be seen that the former presents the appearance of a cone with its base farthest from the eyes, and that the latter presents the effect experienced when looking through a tube.

The illusion of size is apparent by comparing the circle A with the circle B, when it will be seen that although the diameters of both are identical, yet the mind appreciates A as the smaller of the two.

It is difficult to define with any degree of certainty the cause of this illusion. There is obviously a change in the eyes' axes as the attention is turned from A to B, but this does not necessitate readjustment of the optical combination. Once having placed the view at a suitable distance for distinct vision, no further adaptation of focus will be required. Hence we know that the images of the two circles, A and B, are projected upon the retina, identical in size. This leads us to suppose the existence of some power in the mind which dominates over the visual faculties, leading the observer to appreciate retinal impression, not merely from the area of excitation, but also with some regard to mental calculations.

In other words we might say the mind previously disciplined under the set laws of perspective and mathematical rules, refuses to estimate the dimensions of a retinal impression entirely from the points of stimulation.

In the stereoscope, B perspectively represents the interior of a long tube, and the conditions are to all practical purposes identical with nature. In nature the further end of a tube would appear smaller than the end closer to the eyes, but previous education of the mental faculties informs us that the nearer end is only apparently larger than the other, and that if we resort to tangible means of measurement, applying a twelve-inch rule, we shall find the diameter of both ends to be the same.

Thus B, binocularly viewed by means of the stereoscope, fully supports the idea such as would be formed in the mind when looking through a tube in the natural manner. Similar remarks might be made in reference to the cone which is seen.

The explanation thus advanced is that, under certain conditions, the physical energy is made subservient to more powerful exertions of the mind.

Sir David Brewster drew a diagram similar to the accompanying figure, which, however, consisted of only three sets of circles instead of four, as in the present instance; and after observing the apparent inequality of the small circles, he states that the illusion corresponds to that in nature, when the moon appears of different dimensions according to her position in relation to the spectator.

The Stereoscope as an Optical Toy.—The ordinary American stereoscope can, by a simple method, be employed to effect the same purpose as the cinematograph, the wheel of life, and similar instruments. Natural effects of simple actions can be produced, and the stereoscope thus turned into an interesting optical toy.

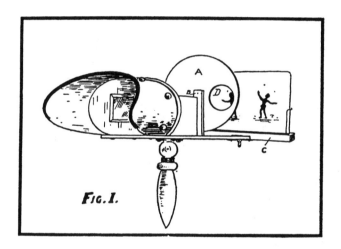

FIG. I.

A disc of cardboard, A, Fig. 2, is cut out, and a circular aperture, D, made in it. The sizes of the disc and aperture are indicated in Fig. 2.

This disc is now pivoted through its centre to the part B of the stereoscope (Fig. 1), so that it will be free to revolve on its axis. If cut to the size indicated, and pivoted high up on B, it will just escape touching the bottom of the stereoscope.

Two pictures, representing two different actions of the same thing or subject, are now photographed or drawn or painted on a plain card of the same size as an ordinary stereoscopic photograph. A card so prepared is shown in Fig. 3. It will be seen that in the left-hand picture one boy is hitting at another, who is attempting to parry the blow ; and in the right-hand picture the boy, who in the first case was parrying the blow, is delivering a blow himself, whilst the other boy is guarding himself.

Other suitable subjects are :—A blacksmith striking a hot iron—in which case one picture would represent him with the hammer raised, and the other with it just striking the anvil—a sea-saw, a juggler with balls (as in Fig. 1), a man on a bicycle, etc.

The following points about these pictures must be noticed :—The distance between the centres of the two pictures or silhouettes must

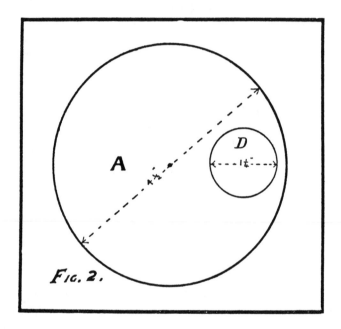

Fig. 2.

not exceed two and seven-eighths inches, and they should be drawn towards the top of the card as in Fig. 3. This latter precaution is necessary in order that the pictures may come opposite the opening D in A, which opening is necessarily high, because the size disc required makes it necessary that its centre should be almost at the top of the division or partition B, Fig. 1.

If now, a card prepared in the manner described—as that shown in Fig. 3, for instance—is placed in the proper holder of the stereoscope, and the disc caused to revolve at a low speed by means of the finger, a person looking through the instrument would see two boys fighting.

The explanation is this:—In an ordinary wheel of life, or cinematograph exhibition, the effect of motion is produced, or imparted by successive presentations to both eyes, of figures as they would appear at different stages. But in the present case the effect of motion is produced by viewing with one eye at a time one of the attitudes of the figures. The right eye, for instance (when the subject of a blacksmith striking an anvil was being viewed), would see the hammer raised, and the left eye would see it lowered in contact with the anvil.

When the disc revolves, therefore, only one picture (either the right or left) is visible at the same moment through the aperture in the

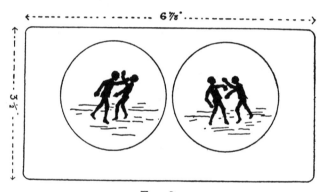

FIG. 3.

disc—the left picture to the left eye, and the right picture to the right eye; and, by the action of the refracting lenses of the stereoscope, both are seen at the same point and plane, just as a pair of dissimilar or stereoscopic photographs would be.

Life-like actions are thus simply obtained by the employment of a stereoscope, with the disc A pivoted to it, and a number of suitably prepared pictures.

Instrument for Teaching the Laws of Binocular Vision.—The movement and various changes that take place in the human eye when looking from one plane to another are exceedingly complex. Beside the actual turning of the eyes under muscular control, each separate eye undergoes that change known as accommodation, which may be taken to mean focusing upon the retina the image of the object to which the eye is directed.

‿ By many direct experiments I have found the following changes to take place in binocular vision, when directing the eyes from a distant object to a nearer one :—1. Both eyes turn inwards, until their axes cross exactly at the point where the object of attention is situated.

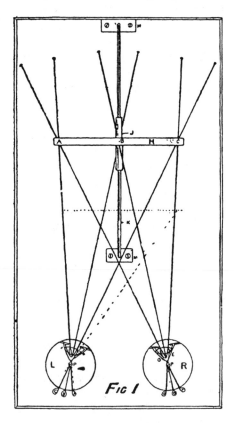

2. The iris of each eye contracts. 3. The ciliary muscles acting upon the crystalline lenses cause them to become more convex, and, consequently, of a shorter focus.

The reason for such changes could be easily accounted for ; but as the object of this article is to describe an instrument with which these changes may be demonstrated, I shall not attempt their explanation here.

The accompanying illustration, Fig. 1, shows the plan of an instrument which I venture to think would prove of some service in science schools, for the purpose of teaching the laws of binocular vision.

I will first describe the instrument itself, and then refer to its teaching capabilities. The base on which the model is mounted consists of a polished mahogany board about $\frac{1}{4}$ in. thick, and bevelled off at the edges. Four brass balls screwed to the underside form the legs (one of these is shown at S, Fig. 3). Two discs of thin brass, L and R, Fig. 1, represent the two eyes, and these revolve on centre screws, P P, fixed to the board. Six wires are then employed to represent oblique and direct rays of light entering the eyes ; these wires also turn on the centre screws P P. To each of the outer wires —*i.e.*, those representing the oblique rays, a metal arm, as shown at D, is soldered, the object of which is to represent the inner portion of the iris in each case—viz., in the right eye R ; the metal arm D is

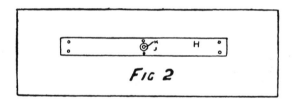

F_{IG} 2

soldered to, and works in unison with, the wire representing the oblique rays emanating from C, whilst the arm E works in conjunction with the oblique rays proceeding from A. The other portions of the iris extending to the circumference of the discs are painted upon the metal. The crystalline lens is represented by thin steel wire, fixed at F F, left eye L. It will be seen that the wires forming the rays extend in both cases to the circumference of the discs at the back, after being once wound around the centre screws P P.

The object to be examined by the eyes is shown at H, and consists of a beam of hard wood pierced with six holes (see Fig. 2) and fitted with a tube J, at the centre. The movement of this beam is controlled by a steel rod, K, Fig. 1, passing through the centre tube J, and supported in the manner shown in the side view, Fig. 3. As will be seen by reference to Fig. 3, this arch-shaped steel support acts as a guide for the beam of wood, and keeps it from touching the surface of the board. Such an instrument may be called an automatic instructor, for we may slide the object H to any distance within the range of the instrument, and the mechanical changes that take place have a fair correspondence with those which the human eyes undergo during their movement and accommodation called for in binocular vision.

Now in reference to its teaching capabilities. Let the student suppose the observer to be looking at an object situated at B, the axes of both eyes will meet at that point, as indicated by the present adjustment of the instrument. On bringing the object H nearer to the eyes until it reaches the dotted line, the following changes will take place. Both eyes will turn inwards, revolving on P P. The oblique wires will diverge, and the size of the supposed image upon the retina will become larger, as indicated by the dotted lines in the left eye L. The irises will have contracted, whilst the crystalline lenses will have become more convex. On shifting the object H to the end of the slide, so that it is further from the eyes, the order of these changes

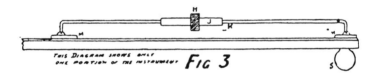

This Diagram shows only one portion of the instrument. FIG 3

will be reversed. The eyes will diverge their axes, the image space upon the retina will become considerably smaller, whilst the irises will be dilated and the crystalline lenses flattened. Hence the apparatus will demonstrate to the student axial movement and accommodation, such as binocular vision demands.

The above article was first published in "The English Mechanic and World of Science," and afterwards fully reviewed in "The Dioptric Review," the Editor, J. H. Sutcliffe, Esq., F.R.S.D., criticising it in the following kindly terms : "The design of this instrument, certainly an ingenious one, has primarily intended it for use in the more advanced Board Schools to demonstrate the laws of binocular vision. The apparatus clearly shows axial movement and accommodation, and although it, in its present state, does not demonstrate the finer points of the actual convexity of the lenses, and the action of the ciliary muscles, we can certainly say that it is calculated to admirably fulfil the purpose for which it was designed."

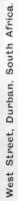

PLATE 14.

West Street, Durban, South Africa.

(*See page* 90)

The Stereo-Triposcope.—As its name implies, this instrument, which is really a modification in pattern of the ordinary American stereoscope, is designed for the examination of three dissimilar pictures of any one object, the centre picture serving first as left eye picture and then as a right, according to its position. The view carriage, A, may be used on the extending arm of an ordinary stereoscope

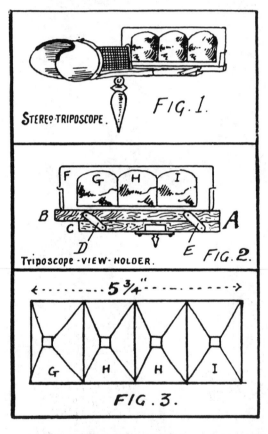

STERE⁰·TRIPOSCOPE.   *FIG. 1.*

Triposcope·VIEW·HOLDER.   *E FIG. 2.*

FIG. 3.

(Fig. 1). It is composed of two beams of wood, B and C, having a parallel motion regulated by two metal links, D and E. Thus it will be seen that, if a tripograph, F, be placed in the holder, and the latter is placed as shown in the diagram, the picture, H, will be that belonging to the left eye, and in the stereoscope it will be coalesced with I. If now the arm, B, is moved in the parallel direction from left to right, G will form the picture for the left eye, whilst H will now be that suitable for the right. It is obvious from this that objects photographed from three different view-points can be examined stereoscopically from two binocular view-points, thus giving the observer a much more comprehensive knowledge of the subject treated. There are many subjects that could with advantage be stereo-tripographed, such as models and complicated pieces of machinery. Such objects can be more completely represented to the mind than ever a single photograph would do, or even a stereograph, for even in the latter case it sometimes happens that some foreground portion completely hides other parts more in the background. It may be urged that the increase in the length of the slide is a drawback ; we would point out, however, that such is only an apparent extension of bulk, for we have here two distinct binocular phases made up only of three pictures. The tripographs may be taken simultaneously by using three lenses, mounted side by side on one camera, at a distance of $2\frac{3}{4}$ inches apart, or the three pictures may be produced successively by shifting a single lens camera an equal distance between the exposures. Simultaneous exposure of the three plates is, of course, absolutely necessary for street scenes or any subjects in motion. For still-life subjects there are several things to be said in favour of successive exposures. Apart from the question of economy, by using the same lens for all three pictures, equivalent magnitude, definition, and density is ensured— points which are sometimes passed as trivial, but which must add something to the sum total of successful work. When a single lens and camera is used for the purpose, it is necessary to see that the axis of the lens points to the centre of the object at each position.

It is curious to note that when mounting the three pictures for the stereoscope, the print taken from the negative made on the extreme right must be placed on the extreme left of the mount, and the print for the negative made on the extreme left must be placed on the extreme right end of the mount. No alteration in the position of the print taken from the middle negative will be necessary ; it must retain its centre position. Unless this transposition of the end pictures is made before mounting, what is known as a pseudoscopic effect will be observed in the stereoscope, i.e., objects that should occupy foreground positions will appear in the remote plane, and distant objects will occupy the foreground. Before passing the subject of two binocular pictures from but three negatives, we might mention how the same end might be accomplished without the special holder already described, reference being made to Fig. 3, by reducing the pictures width-wise, so that four may come side by side within $5\frac{3}{4}$ inches, a stereoscopic slide may be made. Here duplicate prints from one negative (the one taken in the centre) will be required. These are mounted side by side between the other two, G and I (Fig. 3). The views H H, form respectively the companion to G and I. Thus, when using the special slide holder, the two binocular view-points were brought into line for examination by moving the beam, B, in a parallel direction ; but in the latter case the two impressions are gained simply by allowing the axes of the eyes to travel from one combination to the other. It should not be overlooked, however, that in the latter instance two distinct binocular compositions are always visible ; the one not under the more immediate attention being seen obliquely, and the other directly. As long as rays of light emanating from a common point strike corresponding parts of the two retinæ, a single object at that point will be seen, even though obliquely viewed. The combination of the two pairs in Fig. 3 is such that these conditions are fulfilled, with the result of a duplex stereoscopic effect in the mind, the product of both direct and oblique rays striking the retina at corresponding points.

Mechanical Slide for Demonstrating, by the Optical Lantern, the Stereoscopic Field.—As we have already shown binocular vision consists in voluntary and involuntary changes, which take place in the visual organs. The former is a wilful act in turning the eyes in whatsoever direction we please, so that their axes may meet at the point or plane where the object of attention may be situated. The latter is a change or modification in the refracting humours, accompanied with contraction or dilation of the pupil, effected, as we might say, automatically under the influence of light.

The accompanying diagram, Fig. 1, illustrates a mechanical slide which, by the aid of an optical lantern, will serve to demonstrate upon a screen the voluntary changes just mentioned. We will first of all describe the component parts of this slide, and then consider the manner in which it is operated.

The apparatus consists of a framework of wood, fitted with a front and back cover-glass. The black portion in the diagram is cut out of thin wood, and it forms the support on which the model is mounted. This portion, which is glued to the back cover-glass, is supposed to represent the shape of the observer's head when a transverse section

is taken through the centre of the eye balls. The other black portion
at the opposite end of the slide may consist of any thin substance so
long as it is perfectly opaque. The dotted line and reference figures
R, T, P, U, Q, S, I, and J, are painted upon the inside of the cover-
glass. The parts J and I (representing the eyes), with their annexed
V-shaped pieces, are made of celluloid, and are, therefore, transparent.
They are attached to the black support by screws at K and L, on
which they may freely turn when the model is operated. D is a
long metal lever having a slot cut out of it as shown at G, working on
a screw H, fixed to the framework. This lever is connected by rivets

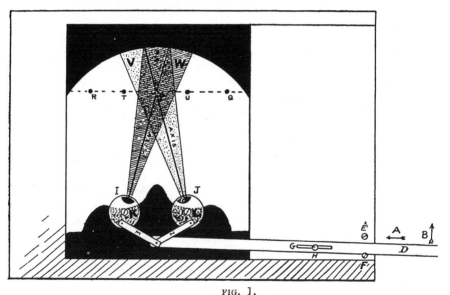

FIG. 1.

to the links M and N, which in turn are pivoted to the eyepieces. The
connection should be sufficiently loose to give perfect freedom when
the slide is operated. Screws fixed at E and F form stops limiting
the movement of the lever. When the portion annexed to J has been
painted a transparent yellow, and the portion annexed to I a transparent blue, the apparatus is complete and ready for exhibition in the
lantern.

We now observe the mode of operating, and the facts this contrivance is capable of illustrating to the audience. Having placed
the slide in the lantern in the ordinary way, the operator controls the

mechanism by means of the lever D. It is obvious that if this lever is raised from its present position and moved in the direction of the arrow B, till it butts against the top screw E, H will act as the fulcrum, causing the opposite end of the lever to drop, taking with it the links M and N, which, in turn, will cause the eyepieces to revolve on the screws K and L, thus the eye J will turn on the screw L from left to right, whilst the eye I will turn on the screw K from right to left, in other words, they will be made to diverge their axes.

The diagram shows the apparatus adjusted for distinct vision of a near object, P, but on causing the movement just mentioned the eyes will be re-adjusted for a remote object situated at S, a point at which the axes will meet.

Let us now suppose that the operator desires to make the eyes look at an object situated at T. He will pull the lever in the direction of the arrow C, at the same time causing the eyes once more to converge to the near plane, by lowering the lever from E to F, and both eyes will be shown to turn from right to left, their axes meeting at the point T. By pushing the lever in the direction of the arrow A an opposite movement will be effected, the eyes will turn from left to right, whilst their axes will meet at the point U. The traversing of the axes along one plane, and their axial accommodation to different distances, will be illustrated.

The apparatus is capable of being put to another purpose also, namely, to show the field covered by both eyes, and that portion covered only by the right eye, and another portion visible only to the left eye. The fact that the shaded portions (that is the V-shaped parts annexed to the eyes) are painted the two tints which together make green, imparts to the overlapping portions that colour, so that in whichever position the apparatus may be placed, that amount of the celluloid presenting a green appearance will indicate the binocular field wherein all parts are seen by both eyes.

The Parallax Stereograms of Mr. F. E. Ives.—To the casual observer these stereograms look like an ordinary bound lantern slide, only it is backed up with ground glass. On holding it in front of a source of light, and at a distance of about twelve inches from the eyes, the subject is seen to have a degree of relief; a very easy matter to understand when explained. The positive consists of narrow strips derived alternately from the two elements of a stereogram; and in front of this composite positive, but not quite in contact, there is fixed a line screen so adjusted that each eye sees its appropriate set of strips, the other set of strips being cut off by the lines of the screen. From the foregoing details it will be seen that parallax stereograms are dependent for their result on an eclipse system, and the circumstances of such phenomena are explained at length in Brewster's work, " The Stereoscope," Chap. 6.

Harmonographic Stereograms.—My method differs from that of Mr. Ives, inasmuch that I use no intercepting agencies, and my two images are not dissimilar but identical. I can quite imagine some stereoscopic workers saying at once that my method must then be impracticable, for it is demonstrated beyond dispute that to obtain a sensation of relief it is absolutely necessary that the two pictures forming the stereoscopic pair should be dissimilar. Let me tell the reader at once that although my two images are identical, when considered separately, they are rendered somewhat dissimilar in the process of their examination, *i.e.*, by a certain overlapping of parts they are regarded as one, whereas in reality the composition is made up of two.

Before going any further it should be stated that some designs lend themselves better than others for this peculiar blending together. Nos. 1 and 2, Plate 15, are designs especially suitable for producing this binocular phenomenon. These particular designs were made by an instrument somewhat on the principle of Tisley's Harmonograph, but consisting of two pendulums swinging at right angles to each other. Attached to the pendulums in a manner calculated to create the least amount of friction, a cane actuating arm extends horizontally, and at right angles to the pendulum. These two arms meet at one point, where they are united by a needle passing through the two. The needle traced upon a sooted glass the original harmonographs. There are several ways such designs may be made to present solidity. We will mention only three. First: The original design may be copied photographically, and then a paper positive from the negative, bound up with the original, the sooted side inwards, protected by a cover glass, and the positive pasted on the outside opposite the design. Second: The original may be bound up with the sooted side facing a mirror. The latter will thus duplicate the original, and this at a plane removed from the real design. Third: The original may be bound up with a transparency made from the negative. In either case a thick mask must be placed between the glass, so that the soot is prevented from coming into contact with the cover glass.

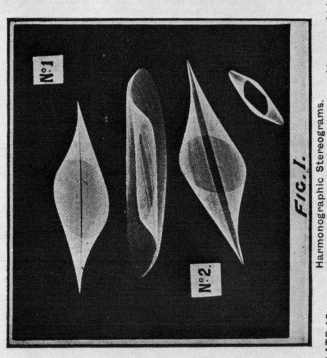

No. 1.

No. 2.

FIG. 1.

PLATE 15.   Harmonographic Stereograms.   (See page 64.)

When the first and second methods are resorted to, the design will be seen stereoscopically when examined by reflected light. In the latter case the relief will be seen by transmitted light. It is interesting to note that in addition to the stereoscopic effect thus produced, the combination, when tilted slightly, gives a mother-of-pearl effect. The causes of these phenomena are not, I think, difficult to assign. Suppose we take two pieces of glass, E F, and G H, Fig. 2, and draw a square on both of equal dimensions, and then bind them up after the manner of a lantern slide, so that one image is removed from the other about one-eighth of an inch. Now, if we hold this a few inches away from our eyes, and parallel to the same, the image projected upon the retina of the left eye, L, will be as A, Fig. 3, whilst the image in the right eye will be as B, Fig. 3. This arises from the fact

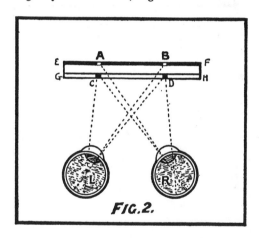

FIG.2.

that C, A, D, Fig. 2, covers all that is seen by the right eye, and C, B, D covers all that is seen by the left. A combination in the stereoscope will give a solidity such as would be produced when looking at the inside of a box. In Fig. 4 we have a reduced pair of pictures. By placing a postcard at right angles to these dissimilar images, so that the arrow is covered by the edge of the card, and each eye can only see one picture, the two will be seen as one, giving the result just mentioned. In other words, we may say that the phenomenon is due to the fact that the white lines composing the designs become merged into each other. In the diagram Fig. 2, B is visible only to the left eye because it is hidden behind D, but when two transparencies are considered, we should say that D and B are by the right eye

F

regarded as one. A false appreciation of two lines as one takes place in both eyes simultaneously, and over the whole combination, with the result of apparent solidity.

Binocular Harmonographs.—I have constructed a compound harmonograph which, by its duplicate needle points, etches simultaneously a pair of dissimilar figures. When examined in the stereoscope these figures are seen as a solid image of exquisite beauty, sometimes possessing a further charm by their defractive power of exhibiting the colours of the solar spectrum.

Stereoscopic View of the Moon.—The dissimilar phases of the moon necessary to give the desired relief are secured by taking

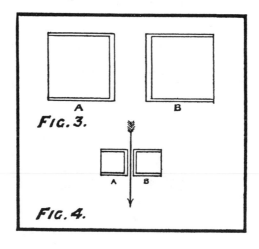

advantage of her libration. Thus, the moon's motion of rotation being uniform, whilst her motion in her orbit is sometimes faster than at others, we sometimes see a few degrees more of her eastern side, and at other times a few degrees more of her western side, and owing to the obliquity of her axis to the plane of her orbit, her north and south poles come alternately into view. Photographs taken at the two extremes give pictures sufficiently dissimilar to produce a perfect sphere when examined in the stereoscope, whilst the mountain projections and the crater depressions are easily discernible.

A Retina Fatiguing Phenomenon and Binocular Illusion.—To the casual observer it would seem that the sensation of solidity in

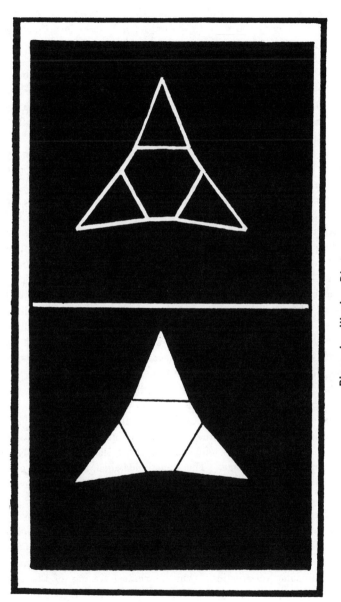

Binocular Illusion Diagram.

(See page 67.)

binocular vision was the result of the dissimilar retinal impressions being simultaneously conveyed to the brain; but closer investigations show that these dissimilar pictures on the retina are regarded, not both at the same moment of time, but separately and alternately. That the retina of either eye may become fatigued has often been demonstrated. The theory of accidental, or what is perhaps better known as complementary colours—the alternate appearances of positive and negative images—and the temporary blindness or insensibility of the retina after the eye has been exposed to excessive light: all substantiate the accepted view, that the activity of the visionary nerves is limited to a definite period, and that the retina is only able to recover its normal sensitiveness after a time of rest.

If we examine the accompanying diagram in an ordinary stereoscope some of the effect we have just mentioned will be apparent. The negative and positive being properly focused and superimposed by the refracting lenses of the instrument, a semi-transparent effect will be noticed in the combined images. This crystallised appearance cannot, however, be retained by the observer beyond a certain period, for after a few moments' observation either a positive or negative image will be seen. There will be a continual change from negative to positive and positive to negative, whilst the intermediate stage will give the semi-transparent or crystallised image already referred to. Such an alternate appearance of positive and negative images is due to the successive fatiguing of the retina in each eye.

If, for instance, we close the left eye, the retina of the right eye will be stimulated with rays emanating from the negative image on the right hand side. On suddenly opening the left eye again (which has been resting from light altogether, and thereby increasing its sensitiveness) we shall see, not as might be expected, the semi-transparent image, but a positive image. The same holds good, but in a reverse order, if we rest the right eye in the first instance, and afterwards use both.

The foregoing experiment is most successfully carried out by having both negative and positive images equally illuminated with reflected light, and the semi-transparent image is best produced if, after adjusting the focus of the instrument, both eyes are closed for rest previous to the binocular observation. The alternate fatiguing of the two retinæ, so clearly demonstrated by the accompanying diagram in the stereoscope, seems to suggest to me a theory that binocular vision consists not merely in a continual accommodation of axial and focal adjustments, but also in the alternate exhaustion of the retina's sensibility. Thus, the use of a second eye is not only necessary to enable the observer to accurately estimate the distance and size of objects before him, but also for supplementing the fading image on the retina of one eye with one growing in intensity in the other, giving as we may term it a perpetual or continuous vision.

Every one knows that in the case of the cinematograph the appearance of motion is produced by the rapidity of successive projections being quicker in their change than the fading of the last image from

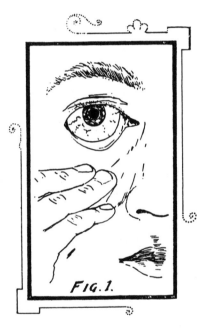

FIG. 1.

the retina. Such a mechanical performance, though clever, is crude indeed as compared with the exquisite provisions of nature within the human eyes. The process of the mind regarding pulsations first from the left eye's optic nerves, and then from the right, furnishes the philosopher with a divine phenomenon beyond his powers of explanation.

Stereoscopic and Panoramic Camera Obscura.—This instrument, invented and described by the author in the "British Journal of Photography" for April 5th, 1901, consists of a camera fitted with a mirror for reflecting upwards a full size binocular picture, which is received upon a horizontal ground glass screen. The lens is furnished with a stereophotoduplicon (described on page 22) which transposes the two images, so that they are received upon the screen in their proper order for immediate examination. Over the screen a collapsible hood is fixed, provided with a pair of prismatic lenses. On looking through these lenses, the observer sees a combination of the dissimilar pictures upon the screen in natural colours and stereoscopic relief, whilst by giving the camera a turn a panoramic effect is produced.

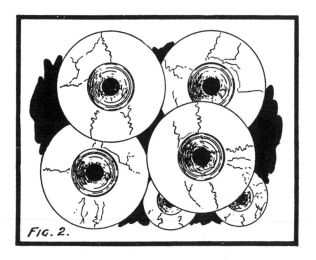

FIG. 2.

A Reliable Means of Identification.—It is strange that, amongst the various means on record for the identification of prisoners and others, we do not find the vein markings of the human eyes resorted to as a guide.

Although, under ordinary circumstances, few of these vein markings are visible, by removing the eyelids in the manner shown in Fig. 1 we discover upon the sclerotica quite a number of these blood veins, some of them are very prominent, especially on the upper half of the eye, *i.e.*, behind the top lid. Their course is generally zigzag, branching off at sharp angles similar to lightning. No two eyes may be found in which the markings are identical, hence the means of distinguishing one person from another.

After carefully registering the markings on certain eyes, some of which are illustrated in Fig. 2, we have found that such markings are not, as might have been supposed, subject to any radical change. Now, it is obvious that, by the aid of photography and various other means, we may make such copies of a person's eyes as would prove a certain and reliable guide to identification at any later date.

Mechanical Science Slide.—By the aid of a mechanical diagram, forming a slide for the optical lantern, most of the changes that take place in the human eye, as it adapts itself for distinct vision of objects situated at various distances, may be clearly shown to an audience. The diagram shows a sectional view of the eye, and the manner in which an object is projected upon the retina.

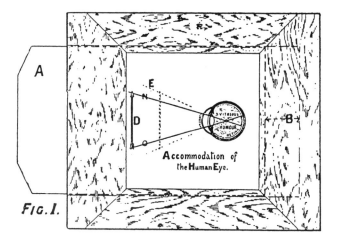

Although there is no attempt to show the exact refractibility of the various humours, those changes in accommodation most noticeable are affected by the mechanism of the slide. On pushing in the sliding glass A, Fig. 1, the object D is brought closer to the eye, and is made to occupy the position of the dotted lines at E. The steel rods N and O (representing oblique rays) being in communication with the other parts cause the iris to contract, the crystalline lens to become more convex, and the image upon the retina to become enlarged.

By drawing out the sliding glass A, again, these changes are reversed in order. Now, I think a slide capable of demonstrating accommodation to the extent intimated should be of some value to every lecturer on subjects pertaining to light, sight, and optics, and for this reason I will venture to give such details as will enable a model to be made by any Optician who desires to do so.

It would be superfluous to go into the details of the framework, it will suffice to say it is made of some kind of hard wood, is provided

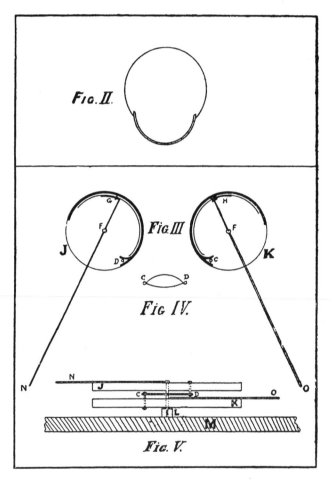

with a rebate on one side to receive the fixed glass (forming a support for the model), and a groove indicated by the dotted lines, in which a second glass A may freely slide backwards and forwards, its play being limited to the space between the arrows at B.

As all the parts, with the exception of the object D, are either painted upon, or are in contact with the fixed glass, this portion of the model may be fitted together before it is placed in the framework. This glass on which the model is to be mounted consists of an ordinary lantern plate, fixed in the hypo bath and washed without having been exposed to light, so that a clear film upon a glass support is obtained. When quite dry, the portion of the diagram, shown in Fig. 2, is drawn upon the film with an ordinary bow pen and Indian or China black ink. These parts are supposed to represent the cornea and the sclerotic coat, and any lettering or reference figures may also be drawn on the film.

Two discs of film, Fig. 3, J and K, also made transparent in the manner just described, are used in the composition of the choroid, the retina and other parts.

The discs are marked as shown in the diagram, and then pierced with holes at F and D in J, and F and C in K, and a rod of steel wire is securely fastened to each, as shown at N and O, extending in each case from the centre of the discs.

The crystalline lens may be represented by a double bow of fine steel wire with a loop at each end, as shown in Fig. 4. All the parts may now be connected together, and, in order to make this operation quite clear to the reader, an enlarged drawing of the arrangement (Fig. 5) has been given. Reference being made to this diagram, a round block of hard wood L, is first glued to the film side of the glass M, this is to form a centre support for the model.

The double bow of steel wire constituting the crystalline lens is now pivoted between the two discs J and K, one pivot passing through the loop C into the lower disc K, and another pivot passing through the loop D into the upper disc J. A small washer should be inserted between the two discs in the centre, in order to keep them sufficiently apart to give the lens and the wire rod O, room to move freely. The model finished thus far may now be inserted into the rebate made in the back of the wooden framework. All that remains to be done to complete the apparatus is to provide the sliding glass A, Fig. 1, carrying the object D.

This object, in the shape of an arrow, consists of a narrow strip of hard wood, with a hole pierced sideways and at each end. Having secured it by means of glue to the inner surface of the sliding glass A, it is slipped into the groove provided for its reception, the two steel rods N and O are threaded through the holes made in the object under observation, and the slide is complete and ready for exhibition.

When projecting such a diagram upon the optical magic lantern screen, its mechanism is so adjusted that it has the appearance shown in Fig. 1, *i.e.*, with the object as far away from the eye as the slide will permit.

After the necessary explanation and remarks have been made, the glass A is pushed in by the operator at the lantern. The object D will thus be brought nearer to the eye, whilst the other changes will be effected. The lecturer or science teacher will thus be enabled to demonstrate in a clear and convincing manner scientific facts, which otherwise would take many words to explain.

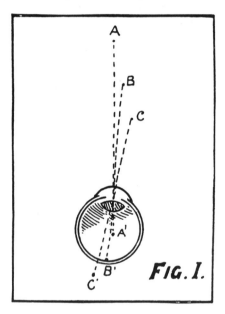

FIG. I.

An Accommodation Slide for the Lecturer.—It is one thing to acquire knowledge, and quite another to impart it, and the latter is the work of the lecturer.

To be successful, the means employed should be convincing rather than elaborate, and to convince an audience I suppose the first essential is clearness. Simplicity here applies alike to words and experiment with apparatus.

Lecturing recently on the subject of " Our Eyes and their Use," I found that apparatus previously constructed expressly for the purpose afforded me the means, not only of securing undivided attention, but also of illustrating in a most convincing manner the statements I found occasion to make.

This demonstrated usefulness induces me to give a brief description of one of the appliances I found especially handy, with the hope that it may prove of service to others.

The apparatus in question is shown in Figs. 2 and 3 : but, before fully describing this, let me direct the reader's attention to Fig. 1. It

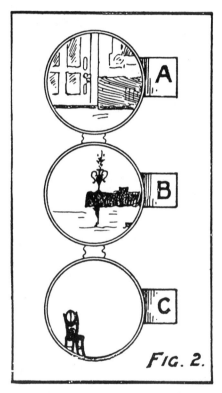

FIG. 2.

is a well-known fact that, in order to see an object clearly, its image must be brought to a focus upon the retina of the eye, and this cannot be accomplished without that change termed accommodation.

If the object of attention be situated at B (Fig. 1) with its image in focus upon the retina at B 1, the image of an object situated closer to the eye at C, will be brought to a focus behind the eye at C 1, whilst the image of an object situated at A will be brought to a focus too soon for distinct vision, and will be within the eye at A 1.

By accommodation the eye is capable of bringing each of these objects in focus upon the retina in succession. The objects out of focus, however, are not entirely lost to view, and their varying degree of clearness, according to their distance from the eye, contributes to that visual combination produced in the mind of the observer, so essential to a general knowledge of his situation in relation to his surroundings.

Although the object of this article is not to point out the changes in the optical combination of the eye when viewing objects at different distances, it may be interesting to note that, if the aperture of the iris and curvature of the lens be such as shown in Fig. 1, page 73, on turning the attention to the foreground object, C, the iris will contract, the pupil become smaller, whilst the lens will take a more convex form. The order of such changes will be reversed if the attention be turned from the nearest object, C, to the remote object, A.

Now it is obvious from these facts that the picture projected upon the retina must be an ever-changing one, with regard to the focus of objects in the view, to say nothing of their varying position caused by divergence and convergence of the axes when both eyes are used.

Were it possible, then, to view the ever-changing picture on the retina of a person's eye under the changes of accommodation, what kind of a picture should he see ? This question is duly answered, and the effect demonstrated by means of what I have called "an accommodation slide."

This slide is to be exhibited in an ordinary single optical lantern, and the projection upon the screen will be a representation of the retinal picture when the eye is brought under the influence already mentioned.

Objects situated at three different planes, A. B, C (Fig. 1), are painted upon three separate pieces of glass. Reference being made to Fig. 2, suppose the remote plane to be occupied by a door, wall, and picture frame, A. The nearest plane occupied by a chair, C, and half way between the chair and the opposite side of the room, a table stands, upon which is placed a vase of flowers, B.

These three glasses are now fitted into suitable framework, such as shown in Fig. 3. The middle glass, B, is fixed, but the two outside ones, A and C, have space to move backward and forward along the groove, the object of which will be pointed out presently.

The objects are painted upon those surfaces of the glasses indicated by the arrows. The distance between A and B should be about a quarter of an inch, whilst the difference between B and C should be rather more. The slight difference in separation of the objects will, in use, correspond with the greater in accommodating the eye from two distinct near planes, and that necessary for accommodation when directing the attention successively to and from two distinct remote planes.

If the slide is now placed in the lantern in the usual way, it is clear that only one of these objects will be in focus upon the screen at the same moment, and that either chair, table, or wall, may be brought into focus at will.

The combined effect will thus be similar, if not identical, to that produced in the eye under natural circumstances, the attention of the observer always supposed to be directed, or adapted, to that object or plane which happens to be in focus upon the screen.

Needless to say, to ensure the best results there should be some intelligent communication between operator and lecturer.

If accommodation is all that the lecturer desires to illustrate, the

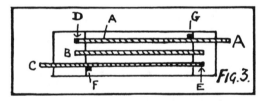

FIG. 3.

three glasses may be fixed; but, should he wish also to show the dissimilar pictures of the retina of each eye under conditions of binocular vision, he may do so by leaving the spaces, E and D (Fig. 3), so that the two outside glasses may be shifted. This movement will, of course, alter the relative position of the objects situated at different planes.

When demonstrating this difference in binocular pictures, the operator should first make B his focal plane, so that a fair amount of clearness may be distributed over the three dimensions of the view. Then, with the three glasses in the position shown in the diagram, the objects as situated from the left-eye standpoint will be shown, and, by pushing the two outside glasses to the end of the grooves, a representation of the right-eye view will be obtained, the movement of the shifting glasses being regulated in the first instance by the stop blocks, F and G, glued to the surface of the glasses; and, in the second instance, by the depth of the grooves, E and D.

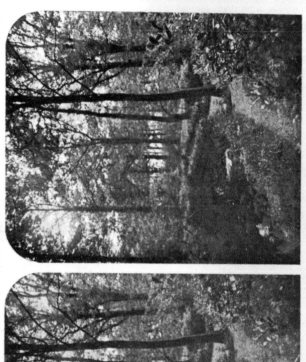

PLATE 16.

Barrow Falls, Cumberland.

(See page 90.)

The Photographic Camera as an Accessory to Lecturing.—There is always a danger of confusing our audience if we use a string of technical terms and calculations, without supplementing such with practical demonstration. This is particularly true when we are treating the subjects of optics.

The photographic camera has often been compared with the human eye, and, indeed, its structure and function are very similar, so that, roughly speaking, we may say: What the photographic artist is able to do by means of his camera, plates, and chemicals, every common

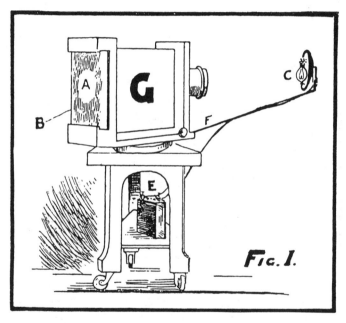

Fig. 1.

observer instinctively accomplishes by means of the eye, nerves, and brain. Hence it is not surprising so many refer to this particular instrument when they wish to illustrate " what we see and how we see it."

Thus, assuming that the lecturer has so made use of these comparisons, we next consider how he may utilise his instrument still further for demonstrating to his audience the truth of his remarks. Let us select that condition of vision known as long sight, illustrating the defect and the remedy. For this purpose we require a large camera G (Fig. 1), dimensions according to size of our audience. The camera is attached to a substantial table or stand by means of the ordinary T screw. It is connected in this manner so that it may be swivelled round at different stages of the experiment. A long rod F, shown in all three diagrams, is now fixed to the front of the camera, so that it moves with the camera as the latter is turned. At the end of this rod an incandescent electric lamp C is fixed, deriving its current from an accumulator E (Fig. 1) placed in a suitable position underneath the table or stand.

The screen B consists of a piece of ordinary ground glass, rather wider than the back of the camera, so that it may be readily withdrawn and replaced at will.

Having so arranged his apparatus and provided himself with a double convex lens D (Fig. 3), the lecturer is ready for his public

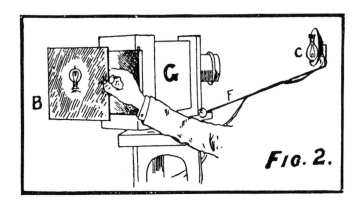

demonstration. The light in the hall is turned low, and the electric light C switched on. The camera being so placed with the screen B turned towards the audience, a blurred image of the lamp C will be seen on the screen at A, Fig. 1. "Ladies and gentlemen," says the lecturer, " having observed the similitude of the photographic camera to the human eye, we shall now endeavour to illustrate by means of this apparatus some of the phenomena of sight. In the first instance, please regard the camera as it is now adjusted as a long-sighted eye. A long-sighted eye cannot see near objects clearly because the rays are not brought to a focus soon enough, the humours not being sufficiently dense. Hence we observe a blurred image of the lamp upon this screen." (Here the camera is swivelled round to give every spectator a proper view of the image.) " Now, if such is the case, we shall find the distinct image somewhere behind the eye ; with the present apparatus, somewhere behind the screen." (Here the ground glass is withdrawn from the camera and gradually moved towards the audience, until the distinct image is found, as shown in Fig. 2.)

"Here" (continues the lecturer) "we discover the distinct image, proving that the refraction of the lens of this camera, which we are regarding as a long-sighted eye, is not sufficient to bring the rays to a focus upon the retina, the screen in its first position." (Placing this ground glass back again into its original position, the lecturer continues.) "This defect of the eye, when it is not accompanied with disease, may be completely remedied by a convex lens, which makes up for the flatness of the crystalline and enables the eye to converge

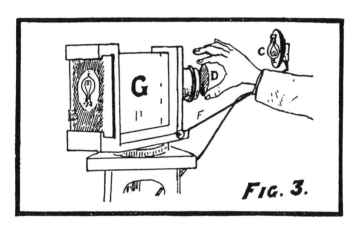

FIG. 3.

the pencils flowing from near objects to distinct foci on the retina." (Here a double convex lens D (Fig. 3) is taken, and held between the lamp and camera lens as shown, when the image of the lamp, hitherto indistinct, is sharply focused upon the screen.)

It is obvious that similar experiments may be made to illustrate various other defects in sight by changing the arrangement of the apparatus and using other forms of lenses.

It should be remarked that, to ensure complete success with the experiment described, the camera should be adjusted previous to public demonstration, so that the lamp C is sharply focused upon the screen when the lens D is held before the camera lens as shown in Fig. 3. By taking such precautions all after-focusing will be unnecessary, and no confusion will result.

Stereoscopic Vision.—There are few people who seem to have sufficient control over the muscles of their eyes to enable them to direct the axes to two separate points and at the same time see such points distinctly. But by a little education or training of the muscles it becomes possible for almost anyone to attain the power. Being able to look at a stereograph stereoscopically is extremely handy when mounting the views, for where is there a stereoscopist who has never made a mistake at this stage of his work ?

It is true, stereoscopic relief may be observed by squinting at the dissimilar pair, but this not only necessitates that the two views composing the slide have to be transposed for the purpose, but the practice is hurtful to the eyes, necessitating, as it does, painful gymnastics of the optical system.

Stereoscopic vision may be regarded as the power to look almost parallel, so that the right-hand view in a stereoscopic slide may be

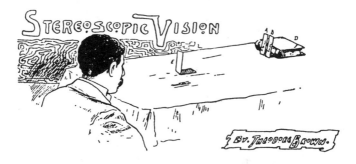

distinctly seen by the right eye and the left-hand view with the left eye, both at the same time, resulting in a combined impression in the mind of the observer.

For the benefit of those readers who wish to learn the secret of stereoscopic vision, I will give a method of training the muscles which I have found to succeed with nine persons out of ten.

The manner of procedure is shown in the annexed cut, but the plan diagram will make everything clear. Cut a strip 1 inch in width out of both the left and right-hand prints of a spare stereogram, leaving them the same height as the original view. The portion selected should contain distant as well as near objects, and the foremost object should occupy the centre position in each strip. Now provide a piece of cardboard (black in preference to any other colour) 1⅝ inches wide and about 6 inches long, bend this at right angles in the centre, so that half may lay flat on the table, whilst the other half will stand perpendicular. Place the two strips of view, A and B, side by side on a table, and resting in a vertical position against a book D. At a dis-

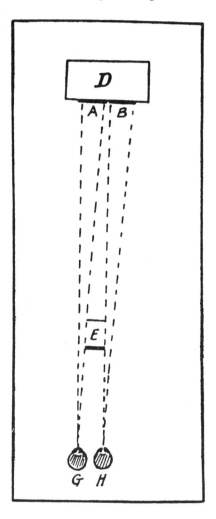

tance of about 3 feet from these strips of view, place the piece of black cardboard, E. The eyes of the observer are then placed at G and H, at a distance from the card E of about 7 inches, and in such a position that the left eye G, sees only the strip A, and the right eye H, sees only the strip B, each eye being prevented from seeing the other strip by the card E.

As the two corresponding points in the views A and B have a separation only of 1 inch, instead of $2\frac{3}{4}$ inches as in ordinary stereoscopic slides, the eyes are easily made to diverge their axes to this slight extent. Having succeeded in coalescing the two strips of view in this position, their separation may be gradually increased by shifting them further apart, until the distance between the two foremost and corresponding points is $2\frac{3}{4}$ inches. This done, you may now substitute the strips of view with an ordinary stereoscopic pair, using the card E until you have sufficient control of the muscles to retain the axes in a parallel direction.

If at any future time it is desired to look at a stereoscopic slide, and some difficulty is experienced, the first and second fingers of the right hand may be held up together at arm's length and made to serve the purpose of the card E.

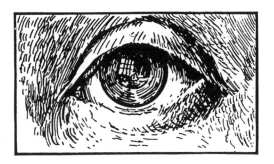

Looking Through the Eyes of Others.—To the casual observer, a photographic portrait furnishes no more than the mean representation of the features taken, but on careful examination by miscroscopic aids, many a photograph will reveal much which otherwise would never have been discovered. Indeed, it is not too much to say that, under favourable circumstances, the photographer may be identified, particulars of the studio given, and the time of day found out, all by the images falling upon the crystalline lens at the moment the photograph was taken.

The accompanying sketch, which is taken from an enlarged photograph, indicates to some extent the possibility of my remarks. The image of a shop window and various objects are seen upon the crystalline lens, which are sufficient proofs that by carrying the experiment to greater perfection much information may be gathered from the pictures visible on the opening of the iris.

To carry the inspection further, a photograph of the two eyes of a person may be enlarged sufficiently to make the spaces on which the image is seen 2½ ins. in diameter. These two enlargements, *i.e.*, a picture of the right eye and also of the left, if mounted side by side and examined in a stereoscope, will present a perfect stereoscopic relief as in Nature, and the observer will thus be enabled to look, as it were, through the eyes (*i.e.*, a copy of the eyes) of the person originally photographed, viewing the same surrounding objects in which the person was situated during the operation.

So perfect is this system of reproducing the images falling on both eyes of the person, that subsequent observers may, by stereoscopic agencies, not only accurately estimate the dimensions of the studio, but also describe the various objects in the view, being guided by the correct proportions and perspective thus given.

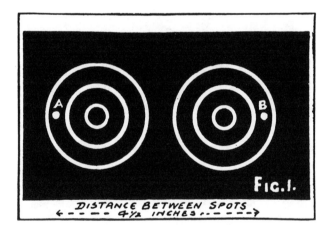

A Binocular Proof of a Blind Spot.—If we make a diagram as shown in Fig. 1, but on a larger scale, so that the distance between the two white spots measures 4½ ins., we shall have a ready means of demonstrating by the stereoscope the fact that the base of the optic nerve is insensible to the presence of light.

The action of the prismatic lenses of the instrument will, of course, present to the mind of the observer a single set of three white circles, and, if the attention be directed to the small centre ring, the observer will be conscious of the presence of two white spots, one on either side of the second ring.

Now, if the axes of both eyes be turned towards the left-hand side spot, the other one will immediately vanish from view, and if, on the other hand, the eyes are directed towards the right-hand side spot, the left-hand spot will vanish.

The plan diagram, Fig. 2, will serve to explain the cause of this phenomenon, thus—if the attention of both eyes are turned towards the right-hand side of the combined image, so that their axes meet

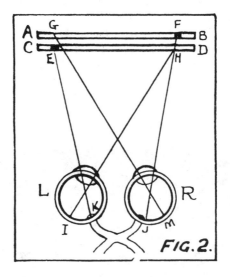

FIG. 2.

somewhere about F and H ; E, which represents the white spot A, of the diagram 1, is visible to the right eye, but not to the left, because in the latter case rays emanating from E fall exactly upon the base of the optic nerve, which is located at K.

Microscopic Stereography.—The subject treated may be photographed from two points of view simultaneously by prismatic transmission, or the dissimilar elements may be obtained successively by a suitable displacement of the lens or subject between the two exposures.

The " Oscillating Stage System " is very convenient and productive of good results, providing the relief is not exaggerated by undue variation in the tilting appliance used. Though not exactly coming under this heading, it may be observed that full size stereograms, obtained in the ordinary way, may be reduced and given a collodion finish for microscopic inspection. The collodion process and oscillating system for stereo-micrography seems to have been adopted for the first time by Dr. R. Z. Maddox, as far back as 1863.

A Stereoscopic Method of Photographic Surveying.—The following method described by Mr. H. G. Fourcade, at the South African Philosophical Society, may be regarded as a mathematical and trigonometrical development of the idea involved in the Grousillier stereoscopic range finder. The essential features of Mr. Fourcade's method may be summed up as follows :

Photographs are taken with a surveying camera, at a pair of points the plates being exposed in the vertical plane passing through both stations. A résean or graduated back frame gives the means of measuring the co-ordinates of any point on the plates with reference to the optical axes of the camera. After developing and fixing, the negatives, or positives from them, are viewed in a stereoscopic measuring machine, which by combining the pictures renders possible the instant identification of any point common to the pair of plates. Movable micrometer wires traverse each field, and pointings may be made simultaneously with both eyes. The readings of the micrometers, referred to the résean, give the three co-ordinates of the point by direct multiplication or division from constants for the plates, constants which depend on the focal length of the lens and the length of the base. When sufficient number of points have been plotted from their co-ordinates contour lines may be drawn.

Visible Direction Diagram.—This diagram, constructed by the author, and shown in the accompanying cut, is intended to illustrate in the stereoscope the laws of visual direction established by Sir David Brewster. The design is engraved upon an aluminium sheet or card of the standard size of stereoscopic pictures. The centre portion marked A, turns on a centre point, so that on moving the indicator B, up and down as the case may be, the arrow on A may be made to point to the left or to the right. Thus when placed in the stereoscope, in its present position, the then single arrow will appear at all points to lie in the same plane as the other portions of the diagram ; but if B is pushed upwards, the head of the binocular arrow will appear nearer to the eyes of the observer than its opposite end ; whilst if B is pulled down, the binocular arrow will point in a direction away from the observer's eyes.

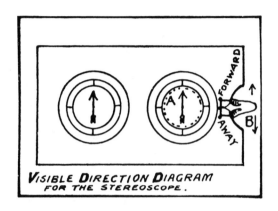

Stereoscopic View of the Eclipse of the Sun.—The eclipse of the sun which took place in the spring of 1901, afforded an opportunity for the production of a stereogram, not without some special interest. During the process of this eclipse the author took two negatives, between the exposure of which the astronomical bodies were allowed to alter their relative positions. The positives thus secured and coalesced in the stereoscope represent the moon as an opaque silhouette disc, in relief, against the luminous disc of the sun.

"The Stereocomparateur."—This instrument, devised by Professor Wolf, of Heidelberg, enables two negatives to be stereoscopically and microscopically compared. By its use the inventor has been able to prove that the stars, when photographed with objectives of short focus, have a measurable parallax, and, further, that in the constellation Berenice there are more than a thousand nebulosities ; Saturn has also been a subject for this microscopic and stereoscopic analysis, with the result that the surrounding satellites of the planet may be seen in their respective planes.

Stereo-Astronomical Charts.—It is easily conceivable, and indeed has been suggested by M. Hamy, that by taking at intervals photographs of a given region of the sky, two successive phases thus obtained may be utilised as stereoscopic elements, which on binocular examination would furnish some very valuable information as to the relative positions and velocity of planets within a specified range.

The Stereoscopic Instantaneous Indicator.—A stereoscopic appliance designed by the author and shown in the accompanying cut, is intended to show without resorting to the stereoscope, whether or not a pair of stereoscopic prints have been properly mounted as regards their relative positions ; or whether two prints from one and the same negative have been mounted side-by side on a stereoscopic mount, and passed off as stereoscopic.

Two plates of clear glass are provided, B and C, the latter sliding in a groove made in the framework, and adjustable as regards its distance from B, by the screen and spring connections F and H. A wooden block D is fixed to the plate C, and provides means of connecting F with the plate C. The frame is provided with a hinged back, which can be opened for the insertions of the prints to be examined. Having inserted a pair of prints, so that they may be inspected from the front

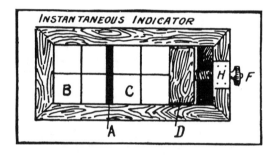

through the glasses B and C, the cross lines upon the glass are made to intersect corresponding foreground objects in the dissimilar pictures. Now supposing the bottom of the vertical and centre line touches a noticeable object in both pictures ; if the dissimilar phases are in their proper order for the stereoscope, a noticeable remote object covered or intersected by the top of the vertical line on B will come a little to the right of the corresponding vertical line in C. If on the other hand the prints still need transposing, then a reverse indication will be apparent.

If on inserting supposed identical prints the vertical and horizontal lines cut through similar part in both pictures, then the supposition will be confirmed. Care should be taken that the two prints examined are always on the same level.

The "Universal Stereoscopic Transposer."—This new printing frame, invented by Mr. W. Rice, is designed to meet the needs of transposition of prints or transparencies from negatives made in twin lens cameras. The accompanying illustrations show the transposer

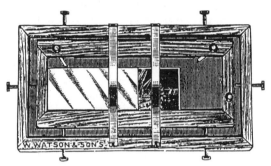

FIG. 1.

with pressure-board removed, and a negative and positive plate in position ready for exposure. As indicated in Fig. 2, the interior portion of the frame is adjustable as regards its position, so that non-perpendicular pictures caused by a side-tilt of the camera during exposure can be connected. This is a very essential provision, for

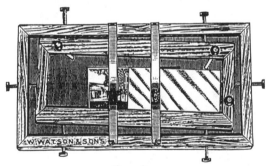

FIG. 2.

unless the dissimilar pair of finished pictures are absolutely on a common level, it is impossible to coalesce them when inspected in the stereoscope.

Motional Direction Illusion Peculiar to Monocular Vision.— That a person having the use of only one eye is liable to this illusion may be demonstrated in the following manner : Take a large bowl of water and place it upon a table. Situate the eyes at an angle of about 90 degrees in relation to the water's surface. Close one eye, and drop a bread crumb into the water, watching it intently with the open eye whilst it becomes saturated with the liquid. As soon as all the air bubbles have escaped from the crumb it will commence to sink, but to the eye of the observer it seems still to float upon the surface of the water, and will appear to be making a sudden move towards him. If now the closed eye is opened, so that both eyes are used, to the surprise of the observer the crumb will be at the bottom of the bowl, and not in the position he had supposed it to be.

Stereoscopic Effects from Duplicate Castings.—If two models cast from one mould are placed side by side, and exactly in the same relative position to a common and plain background ; on being photographed with a single lens, and printed in the usual way, the single print may be examined in the stereoscope, when the prismatic lenses will combine the duplicates and produce a single solid. It should be observed that the operation must be carried out with the axes of the camera lens directed between the two models, and that the background should be placed sufficiently far away from the models as to avoid shadows therefrom ; also, that the distance of the camera from the subject should be such as to bring corresponding points in the duplicate images upon the screen of the camera $2\frac{3}{4}$ inches apart.

REMARKS ON SOME OF THE PLATES.

PLATE 11. THE CLOSE GATE, SALISBURY.—One of the chief diffi-culties of picture making with street subjects is generally the presence of unwelcomed beings who persist in staring straight at the camera. In this picture, however, the camerist has been aided by another artist, who pre-occupies the attention of four little girls, and were it not for the slight disfigurement in the form of a white sunshade, we should pronounce the composition all that could be desired.

PLATE 12. KENSINGTON GARDENS, THE FOUNTAINS.—Had this picture been taken when a subdued light from an overcast sky was falling upon the subject instead of under circumstances of direct sunlight, as here shown, the excessive high tones would have been avoided in a composition eminently suited for stereoscopic treatment.

PLATE 13. INTERIOR, BIRMINGHAM ART GALLERY.—From a technical standpoint this is a very fair specimen of interior work. The reflection of the skylights in the glass dome illustrates in a striking manner a well-known law of optics. The composition is somewhat marred by the unequal lighting of the dissimilar pair of pictures, there being more light emanating from the vase base in the right picture than there is in the left, resulting in an irritating sensation in the eyes when stereoscopically considered.

PLATE 14. WEST STREET, DURBAN, SOUTH AFRICA.—The position from which this picture was taken was well chosen, as the overhanging branch of the near tree supplies a prominent foreground object, which serves to emphasise the stereoscopic effect when binocularly observed in the stereoscope.

PLATE 16. BARROW FALLS, CUMBERLAND.—The country about Barrow Falls abounds in beautiful woodland scenery, such as here shown. We have reproduced the present picture because it contains that quality "atmospheric perspective" so desirable in such a subject. Stereoscopists so often make the mistake of taking woodland scenes when the sun is in the meridian, with the result that the foliage appears to be covered with snow and every drop of water is made a reflector.

THE COMMERCIAL SIDE OF STEREOSCOPY.

THIS heading is comprehensive of three classes of industry. The making and selling of stereoscopic photographs—the manufacture and sale of stereoscopic apparatus—and the writing and publishing of literature on the subject.

MESSRS. UNDERWOOD AND UNDERWOOD, who may be regarded as pioneers in developing public interest in the stereoscopic photograph along educational lines, have built up a system so comprehensive and efficient that the world at large are benefitted thereby.

Their expert operators are at work at every corner of the globe, stereoscopically recording current events of any importance, and securing photographs of places of historical interest.

The magnitude of their business may be understood from the fact that they have beside their stereoscopic factory at Westwood, New Jersey, three plants where stereographs are made. From these enormous stocks of glass-printing machines, located respectively in Washington, D.C., Arlington, New Jersey, and Littleton, New Hampshire, are produced the magic pasteboards. Their main offices are in New York, Ottawa, Kansas, and San Francisco, Canada being supplied from Toronto.

The London warehouse is situated at 3, Heddon Street, Regent Street (by the New Gallery), where an immense stock of views are kept for furnishing goods to the various branches on the Continent as well as local and colonial trade. Their views are issued in sets of 36 upwards, and are put up in boxes the shape of a book. A special guide book has been written, by reliable authors, to go with each set. The guides contain special patented maps, which show at a glance the exact point from which any view in the set was taken; whilst the order of the views are as they were taken on the tour through the countries depicted. In addition Messrs. Underwood and Underwood are the publishers of "The Traveller," a quarterly magazine, devoted to the interest of stereoscopic art, travel, and education. For the benefit of our readers we reprint a portion of the publisher's circular referring to this magazine :—

" The Traveller " occupies a place in the field of magazine literature that is absolutely unique.

The important objects and interesting scenes in every country and in every clime are stereographed by the publishers' skilled artists, who visit the remotest corners of the earth for this special purpose.

No significant event in any nation of the world, no phenomenon of nature that will at all yield to the power of the twin-eyed camera is allowed to transpire without being stereographically recorded and preserved for the readers of " The Traveller," the mission of which is to interpret important events and the most interesting works of nature, art, and human genius in every country in the light of these stereographic records made of them.

> " Sounds which address the ear are lost and die
> In one short hour; but that which strikes the eye
> Lives long upon the mind ; the faithful sight
> Engraves the knowledge with a beam of light."

As it is the province of no other publication to do, " The Traveller " elucidates and familiarises its readers with the wonderful and sublime in every country—" The sights which men risk their lives, and spend their money, and endure sea-sickness to behold " ; it awakens a sympathetic interest in the lives, customs and habits of the various peoples of the world, and stimulates a feeling of kinship with them and desire to know more about them.

Its contributors speak with authority, for they have seen the things of which they write. " The Traveller " will help you to see with them and share their experiences.

It is a sufficient guarantee of the magazine's exceptional literary merit to know that Dr. D. J. Ellison is the Editor.

Its regular contributors are all eminent in their special departments, such as M. S. Emery, art critic of the Prang Company; Professor Chas. N. Crewdson, corresponding secretary of the Society of Egyptian Research ; Miss Keller, recently editor of " Young Folks" ; Mr. Hungerford, associate editor of " Success " ; Professor James Ricalton, one of the greatest travellers now living ; Theodore Brown, of England, one of the very great authorities on binocular vision ; and a large number of noted special contributors.

Yearly subscription, 4s.

W. TYLAR, 41, HIGH STREET, ASTON, BIRMINGHAM.—In the publication of views Mr. Tylar is also doing a good work. His specialities being 12 views in a packet. B.P. series 1/8. Bromo-type series 3/2. He also supplies stereoscopes of various patterns, in addition to stereoscopic cameras.

NEGRETTI AND ZAMBRA, 38, HOLBORN VIADUCT, LONDON, E.C.—This firm has quite a gallery of stereoscopic transparencies on view of the collodion type, and readers who wish to see a stereoscopic transparency of high class quality and finish should pay them a visit.. A stock of stereoscopic apparatus, including cameras and stereoscopes, can also be seen, and they are the English agents for the " Verascope " Camera, and the " Taxiphoto," an elaborate stereoscopic cabinet, by means of which 1,000 views taken in the " Verascope " may be brought under binocular observation without touching the transparencies with the fingers. An indicator is fitted to the side of the apparatus, and by turning a pointer to the number of the view it is desired to see ; on pressing a lever on the opposite side the stereogram comes into line behind the adjustable lenses.

THE FINE ART PHOTOGRAPHER'S PUBLISHING COMPANY.—This company issues a stereoscope named " The Realisticscope," somewhat like the ordinary American pattern, but very highly finished. It has a fixed pedestal stand, aluminium hood, velvet edges, and the prismatic lenses are very carefully mounted, giving perfect parallelism and equality of refraction. With this instrument they are publishing their gold medal series of stereographs, which we recommend as being unsurpassed in technical excellence and finish. The errors mentioned on page 25 have been avoided, the original view points well selected, and the finished prints properly trimmed,

THE LONDON STEREOSCOPIC COMPANY, 106 AND 108, REGENT STREET, LONDON.—This firm originally introduced stereoscopic photography into England on a commercial basis. Sir David Brewster in his book refers to the stock of views then held by this company, which is sufficient to show that they were pioneers in the trade. To-day they supply every appliance for stereoscopic work.

BOOKS.

THE STEREOSCOPE. By Sir David Brewster, contains 235 pages, 52 illustrations, 4s. 6d.; 1870 out of print, but can be seen at the library of the Royal Photographic Society, 66, Russell Square, London.

THE STEREOSCOPIC MANUAL. By W. I. Chadwick. Being a remodel of a short series of papers contributed to the "British Journal of Photography," 1888-89, 1891, 1s. John Heywood, 2, Amen Corner, London, E.C.

THE STEREOSCOPE AND STEREOSCOPIC PHOTOGRAPHY. From the French of F. Drouin. Translated by Matthew Surface, 2s. Percy Lund, Humphries and Company, Country Press, Bradford.

THE ELEMENTS OF STEREOSCOPIC PHOTOGRAPHY. By C. F. Seymour Rothwell, F.C.S., 1896. Being No. 9 of Lund's Photographic Series, 6d.

THE STEREOSCOPE AND STEREOSCOPIC PHOTOGRAPHY. By Oliver Wendell Holmes. 80 pages, no illustrations, gratis of—Underwood and Underwood, 3, Heddon Street, Regent Street, London.

STEREOSCOPIC PHOTOGRAPHY. Edited by John Tennant, 1899. Being No. 5 of the "Photo-Miniature." English agents—Dawbarn and Ward, Arundel Street, Strand, London.

Thomas Bedding, F.R.P.S., Editor of the "British Journal of Photography," on stereoscopic photography in his Photographic Almanack for 1900, devoted about 30 pages to the subject; and The Year Book of Photography for 1902 contains an article of equal length from the pen of its editor, R. Salmon, F.R.P.S., on the "Progress and Practise of Stereoscopic Photography."

INDEX.

A.

C.

97

G.

PAGES.

100

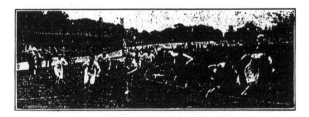

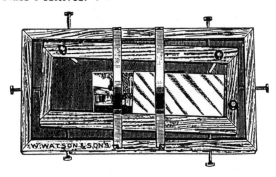

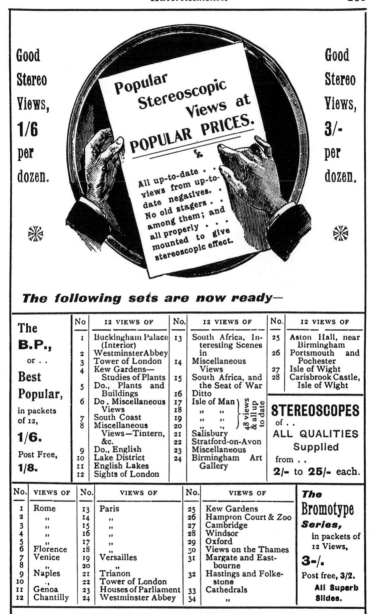

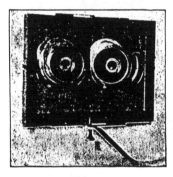
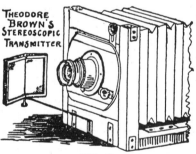

THEODORE BROWN'S
Improved STEREOSCOPIC TRANSMITTER
Is fitted with Anti-Climatic and Untarnishable Spectra.

Fig. 3 shows the Transmitter as used with a Camera having an extending baseboard.

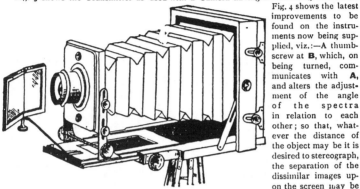

Fig. 4 shows the latest improvements to be found on the instruments now being supplied, viz.:—A thumb-screw at **B**, which, on being turned, communicates with **A**, and alters the adjustment of the angle of the spectra in relation to each other; so that, whatever the distance of the object may be it is desired to stereograph, the separation of the dissimilar images upon the screen may be adjusted to 2⅜ in., the

FIG. 3.

desirable distance between corresponding points in the two images. The iron thumbscrew hitherto used at the junction of the mirrors, to attach the frames to the connecting rod, has been replaced by a more substantial nut and screw, **C**; whilst the connecting rods are supplied with a number of holes made in them, so that the distance of the instrument from the lens of the Camera in use may be modified. Illustrated instructions are issued with each instrument sent out, and the manufacturer is always open to give further assistance by letter, if desired, providing a stamped addressed envelope is sent with enquiries.

**For Specimen Pictures taken,
See Plates 1 & 6.**

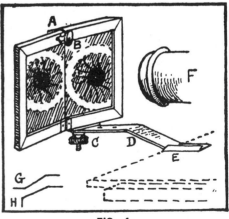

FIG. 4.

Price complete, with full instructions, 10/6, post free.
Outside the United Kingdom, 14/6, post free.
State Maker's Name, Size, and pattern of your Camera when ordering.
SEE FOLLOWING PAGES. ☞

DIRECT FROM—
THE STEREOSCOPIC SUPPLY STORES, 34a, Castle Street, Salisbury.

WHAT ITS USERS SAY,

AND . .

Who can Judge better than those who have had Practical Experience ?

"I am very pleased with your Transmitter, it is a most ingenious instrument."

"I have given the Stereoscopic Transmitter a thorough testing, with excellent results."

"I think your Transmitter will be a distinct acquisition to my outfit."

"Following your instructions, my first negative is indeed very satisfactory."

Such are the expressions in unsolicited testimonials, the originals of which may be seen at the works.

The prediction of the Photographic Press that this instrument would rapidly become a favourite addition to the photographer's kit, is now an accomplished fact. All doubt as to its practical utility has long since been swept away by constant public testimony of those who use it. The Stereoscopic Transmitter, still holding its own against more complicated, expensive, and less successful appliances has gained a prominent position in optical science, and is now recognised as the simplest method of Stereoscopic Photography ever devised. This fact is a sufficient proof that the Stereoscopic Transmitter may be relied upon as an instrument capable of rendering satisfactory results.

Opinions of the Press.

Invention.—"A simple and ingenious little instrument."

The Optician.—"We think that every intelligent photographer who possesses only a single lens camera should become the purchaser of one of Mr. Brown's Stereoscopic Attachments."

The Helios Illustrated International Review of Practical Photography.—"This little instrument, which is very practical, should not have the slightest difficulty in introducing itself into every amateur's kit."

Photogram.—"A useful Transmitter."

British Journal of Photography.—"Effective."

Evening Times.—"A piece of apparatus which should be of interest to all who indulge in photography."

Chemist and Druggist.—"A clever thing for taking Stereoscopic pictures in a single-lens camera."

The British and Colonial Printer and Stationer.—"That this little instrument does its work well we can vouch for, having given it a practical trial with good results."

The Indian and Eastern Engineer.—"A very clever idea for taking Stereoscopic pictures with a single lens, on one plate, and with one exposure."

Photographic Review of Reviews.—"We anticipate a large sale of this Transmitter, as it is eminently practical, and the price complete (10/6) is by no means prohibitive."

Amateur Photographer.—"The Stereoscopic Transmitter is an ingenious little device, perfectly satisfactory."

The Tunbridge Wells Advertiser.—"It is easily attached to, and does not interfere with the ordinary work of the camera."

The Fakenham Times—"District Camera Club Exhibition—Mr. Theodore Brown had on view one of his Stereoscopic Transmitters, by means of which Stereoscopic pictures can be successfully taken with the usual single-lens camera, at one operation, and without alteration of camera or use of twin lenses."

The Photographers' Supplement to the Bazaar, Exchange and Mart.—"In examples we have seen, in which Mr. Theodore Brown's invention has been employed, the Stereoscopic effect has been perfect, while the manipulations required to obtain it are of the simplest nature."

ORDER DIRECT FROM—

THE STEREOSCOPIC SUPPLY STORES,

34a, Castle Street, Salisbury.

THEODORE BROWN'S

... IMPROVED ...

Stereoscopic Adapter.

FOR ILLUSTRATION OF THIS
INSTRUMENT,

SEE PAGE 17, Fig. 21.

Price **5/-,** Post Free.

with full instructions.

THIS is an Apparatus designed expressly for taking Stereoscopic Views with the ordinary single lens ¼-plate Camera.

Being a kind of extra tripod table, and having on its upper surfaces a parallel rule, one rule being fixed to the table and the other to the bottom of the camera employed. Thus, exposures are made in two different positions—one with the camera to the right, and the other, with the camera moved, across to the left side. The prints from these two negatives, when mounted side by side in the same order as they were taken, form the Stereoscopic View, and produce the same effect as that of views taken in the Stereoscopic Camera, the only difference being that, with the Stereoscopic Adapter, two exposures have to be made, or rather, two negatives taken.

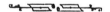

For Sample Stereoscopic View taken by the Improved
Stereoscopic Adapter, See Plate 4.

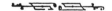

ORDER DIRECT FROM—

THE STEREOSCOPIC SUPPLY STORES,

34a, Castle Street, Salisbury.

PRICE LIST of STEREOSCOPES.

Delivered Carriage Paid to any Address within the United Kingdom
at the following prices:—

AMERICAN PATTERN STEREOSCOPES.

(Similar to Fig. 4.)

FIG. 4.

	£	s.	d.
No. 1—Cherry-wood, folding handle	0	1	6
No. 2—Cherry-wood, plush-edged hood	0	2	6
No. 3—Walnut, plush-edged hood	0	2	9
No. 4—Walnut, large lenses	0	3	0
No. 5—Aluminium, high finish	0	5	6

BOX FORM STEREOSCOPES.

	£	s.	d.
No. 6—Similar to Fig. 1, page 31	0	6	0
No. 7—Ditto, but superior finish	0	8	0
No. 8—Similar to Fig. 2, page 31, with opera glass adjustment	1	1	0
No. 9—Ditto, with best achromatic lenses	1	5	0
No. 10— ,, ,, ,, ,, larger ...	1	10	0
No. 11— ,, ,, ,, ,, very high finish	2	5	0
No. 12— ,, mounted on adjustable pedestal ...	5	18	6

POCKET & COLLAPSIBLE STEREOSCOPES

FIG. 11.

	£	s.	d.
No. 13—Fig. 11, Nickel-plated, Mirror Stereoscope (for further particulars, see page 35)	0	1	6
No. 14—The Reflectoscope (Fig. 10, page 35)	0	2	0
No. 15—Tylar's best Portable (Fig. 7, page 34)	0	1	9

Continued on following pages. ☞

ORDER DIRECT FROM—

THE STEREOSCOPIC SUPPLY STORES, 34a, Castle Street, Salisbury.

PRICE LIST of STEREOSCOPES.

Delivered Carriage Paid to any Address within the United Kingdom
at the following prices:—

STEREOGRAPHOSCOPES.

For viewing Landscape Views, Portraits, or Stereoscopic Views.

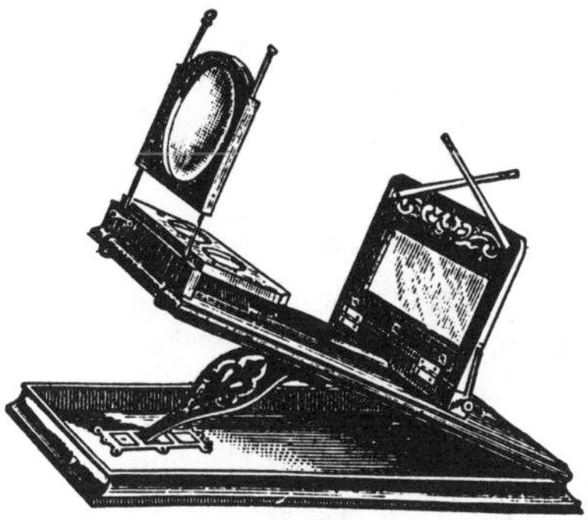

FIG. 13a.

	£	s.	d.
No. 16—Similar to Fig. 13, page 36, in Mahogany, size of large lens, 4⅛ in.	0	15	0
No. 17—Walnut, ditto, size of large lens, 4⅛ in.	0	15	6
No. 18 — Ebonised and flowered, size of large lens, 4⅛ in.	1	0	0
No. 19—Olive Wood and Nickel Mounts, size of large lens, 4⅛ in.	1	0	0
No. 20—Walnut, size of large lens, 5 5⁄16 in.	1	7	6
No. 21—Rosewood, with Fillets, size of large lens, 5 5⁄16 in.	1	11	6
No. 22—Ebonised and Flowered, „ „ 5 5⁄16 in.	1	12	6
No. 23—Olive Wood & Nickel Mounts „ „ 5 5⁄16 in.	1	13	6
No. 24—Walnut or Rosewood, with Fillets „ 6½ in.	2	6	6
No. 25—Ebonised and Flowered, size of „ 6½ in.	2	10	6
No. 26—Olive Wood & Nickel Mounts „ „ 6½ in.	2	10	6
No. 27—Walnut or Rosewood, with Fillets „ 7 1⁄16 in.	3	1	6
No. 28—Ebonised and Flowered, size of „ 7 1⁄16 in.	3	17	6
No. 29—Walnut or Rosewood, with Fillets ., 8 ₄ in.	3	19	6
No. 30—Ebonised and Flowered, size of „ 8¼ in.	4	15	6

Also supplied with oval lenses, from 5 5⁄16 × 4 5⁄16 in.
to 8¼ × 6⅞ in., at proportionate prices.

	£	s.	d.
No. 31—Similar to above, Fig. 13a, Polished Mahogany	3	6	0
No. 32— „ „ in Walnut	4	0	0
No. 33— „ „ larger size	6	6	0

Continued on following pages. ☞

ORDER DIRECT FROM—

THE STEREOSCOPIC SUPPLY STORES, 34a, Castle Street, Salisbury.

PRICE LIST of STEREOSCOPES.

Delivered Carriage Free to any Address within the United Kingdom
at the following prices:—

REVOLVING & MAGAZINE STEREOSCOPES

(Similar to Fig. 3, page 32.)

	£	s.	d.
No. 34—Polished Mahogany, Ebonised Eye pieces, capacity 25 views	1	16	0
No. 35—Ditto, capacity 50 views	2	2	0
No. 36—Polished Walnut, ditto, capacity 25 views ...	2	0	0
No. 37— ,, ,, ,, ·, 50 ,, ...	2	4	0
No. 38— ,, ,. or Rosewood on Plinth, ditto, capacity 50 views	3	3	0
No. 39—Ditto, superior, capacity 50 views	3	18	6
No. 40— ,, rounded corners, capacity 50 views ...	3	10	6
No. 41— ,. ,, ,, superior, capacity 50 views	4	4	0
No. 42—Polish Walnut, octagon corners, capacity 50 views	4	7	6
No. 43—Polished Walnut, double supports, drawer and reflector, capacity 50 views	6	0	0

AUTOMATIC STEREOSCOPE.

No. 44—Mahogany body, for 50 views, allows 12 pictures to be seen each time 1d. is put into the slot, achromatic lenses	4	5	0

SALOON STEREOSCOPES.

No. 45—For 200 views, with large lens for cabinet photos, in Polished Mahogany or Walnut, first quality finish, handles and rack adjustment to lenses, on castors	14	0	0
No. 46—Ditto, ditto, ebonised and engraved	20	0	0

Continued on following pages. ☞

ORDER DIRECT FROM—

THE STEREOSCOPIC SUPPLY STORES, 34a, Castle Street, Salisbury.

PRICE LIST of STEREOSCOPIC SLIDES.

Delivered Carriage Free to any Address within the United Kingdcm
at the following prices:—

No. 47—Plain Views of Paris, &c.   2/- per doz.   21 - per gross

No. 48— „   „ assorted   3/-   „   30/-   „

No. 49— „   „ 1st quality ...   .   3/4 per doz.

No. 50— „   „ extra quality ...   .   5/6   „

No. 51— „   „ of Palaces & Castles, 1st quality   5'6   „

No. 52— „   „   „   „   extra „   8/-   „

No. 53— „   „ of our country, 1st quality ...   8/-   „

No. 54— „   „   „   „ extra „   ...   9/6   „

No. 55— „   „ of Parisian Actresses, 1st quality   6/-   „

No. 56— „   „ of England, English make,
                 1st quality ...   .   8/-   „

No. 57— „   „ of Comic Subjects, 1st quality   8/-   „

No. 58— „   „   „   „   2nd „   6/-   „

No. 59— „   „ Instantaneous, Marine, extra
                 quality ...   .   6/-   „

No. 60—Transparent Views, assorted   ...   ...   4/-   „

No. 61—   „   „ 1st quality   6,6   „

No. 62—   „   „ Artistic Subjects, coloured   10/6   „

No. 63—   „   „ Paris Theatres,   „   27/6   „

No. 64—American manufacture, assorted, plain ...   36/- per gross

No. 65—   „   „ best comic   ...   8/- per doz.

No. 66—Glass, French Stereo Slides, 2nd quality...   2/- each

No. 67— „   „   „   „ 1st   „   ...   5/6   „

No. 68— „ English „   „ 1st   „   ...   3/-   „

Continued on following page. ☞

ORDER DIRECT FROM—

THE STEREOSCOPIC SUPPLY STORES, 34a, Castle Street, Salisbury.

Printed by THE GUTENBERG PRESS, LIMITED, 123, 124 & 125, Fleet Street, London, E.C.